THE
HEALTH
OF
YOUR WEALTH™

YOUR FINANCIAL GUIDE TO WHAT THEY
NEVER TAUGHT YOU IN LAW SCHOOL

HOWARD WOLKOWITZ

WISER CHOICES : RICHER LIFE™

THE HEALTH OF YOUR WEALTH ™

YOUR FINANCIAL GUIDE TO WHAT THEY NEVER TAUGHT YOU IN LAW SCHOOL

ISBN: 978-0-9971042-4-0
Printed in the United States of America

PUBLISHER
HW Media
www.howardwolkowitz.com
howard@howardwolkowitz.com

CONTENTS

PREFACE

This book is dedicated to your most important client: you and the family that depends on you. Whether you are a generalist, a specialist, or an independent practitioner or employed in a practice, you share something with your fellow practitioners. Somewhere on your journey you made a promise that the sacrifices you and your family made would lead to financial security and financial freedom.

You were well trained to protect your family of legal clients, but were you as well trained to protect your own family from the financial challenges of life? All the hard work you invested in studying law was to fulfill the goal of becoming a successful lawyer.

What they never taught you in law school was how to create and implement a business development "state of mind" and a wise financial strategy to help you manage the money you will make as a successful attorney.

Lawyers have long recognized that although they may be technically astute at law, they may not be as adept at the skill of cultivating business. Yet, when you ask which attorneys make more money, have more control of their businesses, have more job security, and command the respect of other lawyers in the firm. The answer is always the same: "business originators." *Create wealth and protect it.*

This book will teach you to:
- **Determine** your ideal balance between work and family.
- **Learn** how to protect your hard-earned assets by creating a wealth team.
- **Evaluate** the quality, cost and value of the financial advice you receive.
- **Minimize** overlaps and waste from the multiple financial recommendations you receive.
- **Integrate** all the financial advice you receive into a successful outcome.

Create a sound investment in your family's future. Break the cycle of financial waste and build long-term financial security. Take control of your financial future by attracting your own clients.

SECTION ONE SUMMARY: FOUNDATION OF WEALTH

The foundation of wealth consists of teams and teamwork. A foundation can be a basis for or a principle behind something. It can be the base upon which a structure sits or it can be an entity like a charity.

You may think about wealth in terms of **safety** (*"I don't want to lose any money."*), **trust** (*"I don't know who to trust with my money."*), **choice** (*"what options are best for me?"*); **collaboration** (*"how do I get my advisors to talk to and work together?"*), and **wisdom** (*"how do I know that the recommendations I took and the decisions I made were wise choices?"*).

When you don't know better, you may accept the recommendations of those who are less qualified to give advice. The less you know and the less confident you are about your own ability to make wise financial decisions, the greater the possibility that you may accept mediocrity in your financial life.

You were trained to be a highly effective practitioner. *The Health of your Wealth* will help show you how to source, create, and manage a highly effective financial team to take the actions needed to achieve results.

- Learn to think about your financial team in a new way.
- Start categorizing your advisors as trustworthy or transactional salespersons.
- Explore how even seemingly inconsequential financial decisions made over a period of time can lead to detrimental or even catastrophic results.
- Discover why financial planning by itself is not enough.
- Read why the key to managing your wealth is managing your risks.
- Learn how to evaluate different types of life insurance policies.
- Learn how to evaluate different types of disability policies.
- Learn how to evaluate different types of long-term care policies.
- Plan for a safe retirement.
- Explore the many types of special circumstances that can impact your finances.

CHAPTER 1
YOUR WEALTH TEAM

"All I wanted since I was in college was to be a lawyer. Now I have become just another billable hour generator for the partners, with no time to think about my finances."

"I bought a life insurance policy from my buddy because I wanted to help him out. I have no idea if that was the right decision. I'm not sure what I own or if it was the right insurance for me."

"I trust that my advisors are doing the right thing for me because I have no idea what the right things are and I have no time to even think about it."

How and whom you trust may be more important to you than the actual financial decisions you make, and may have a larger impact on the quality of your life. The central focus of this book is on identifying and putting your trusted team in place. With the right team in place, financial security and work/life balance is possible. The road to a good quality life and financial wisdom starts with trust, the foundation of all meaningful relationships. It is crucial to establish trust with the right advisors.

Behind every financially successful lawyer, you'll find trustworthy advisors. These professionals are your counselors and confidential sounding boards. A true advisor helps you navigate through your financial fears, blind spots, and concerns.

Law school does not prepare you to manage the money you will make or how to identify competent and capable advisors. By understanding what professional financial advisors do, and by learning about the skills and tools they use, you can do a better job at selecting professionals who can successfully fulfill the role of trustworthy advisors.

Knowing what sources of information and people to trust is the most difficult thing about making financial choices. Where do you start? How many advisors should you interview and how many advisors should you work with? What questions should you ask your advisors and what information do you need? How many investments should you make and how much can you afford to invest? How much risk should you take on? Do you pay off debt first or do you save for a house, car, or retirement?

How can you identify a trustworthy advisor? Preparing yourself to find the right level of support will require you to educate yourself about the criteria used to evaluate these choices.

A trustworthy advisor with vision (and you, yourself) should ask and help answer the following:

- What do you want to accomplish in your financial life?

- Why are these accomplishments important to you?

- When would you like to accomplish these goals?

- How should you manage this process to ensure your goals get achieved on time?

- How much money are you squandering or 'leaving on the table?'

- Where will you gather the information you need to have your dream life?

- Who are the essential people you require to accomplish your goals?

THINK OF YOURSELF AS
A PATIENT CHOOSING A DOCTOR

Choosing a healthcare provider is an important decision. Your relationship with your doctor, whether a primary care physician or a specialist, helps determine the quality of care you receive. The right choice of doctors makes a difference in how you manage your health and overcome disease. You trust your medical doctor to care for your health, to help you make important health-related decisions, to keep up with pertinent medical breakthroughs, and to provide ongoing advice.

An expert in the medical field might be a surgeon who has successfully performed the specific type of surgery you require numerous times. This is the doctor you want doing *your* surgery. Your trustworthy advisor is the financial "doctor" who manages your financial health. An expert in the financial field is someone who has successfully created solutions for others with your particular needs. These are the trustworthy advisors *you* want on your team.

If you had a serious health issue, you would look for a qualified healthcare professional to assist you, even though a primary care doctor could also give you medical advice. With matters as important as your financial health, seek the advice of financial professionals.

If you have trouble trusting yourself, your lack of self-confidence may condemn you to leaning on other people, crossing your fingers, and hoping you make the right decisions. Not having a concrete plan in place; not balancing your short-term, intermediate, and long-term goals; investing too aggressively and losing money; investing too conservatively and not earning enough to achieve your goals; and not having appropriate or sufficient insurance in place when you and your family need it are typical symptoms of not working with the right team of advisors.

The financial care concept presented in this book was designed especially for the legal community. It offers tools with which you can take control of your financial decisions at each stage of your life from law school through retirement.

Develop the knowledge and skills you need to trust yourself. Learn how to identify financial mistakes, how to set up a team of trustworthy advisors, and how to look at risk management. Understand the personal insurance industry and the products it offers, learn how to prepare for a successful retirement, and understand special needs and special considerations.

Together with your trustworthy advisors, you can create a workable plan that supports sound financial decisions. Become an educated buyer of financial products and services and trust yourself to take responsibility for your own financial destiny.

A LAWYER'S DILEMMA: YOU ARE NOT ALONE

The pressure of billing 2000 hours per year reduces the time available to take care of your own needs and financial well being. Questions all lawyers should be answering are:

- How financially prepared do you feel?

- What is your level of personal financial knowledge?

- How confident do you feel about your financial decisions?

- What are your top financial concerns?

- Are your investments on track to create a successful retirement?

- Do you have enough and the right type of insurance protection?

YOUR FAMILY'S FINANCIAL ADVOCATES: WHO'S ON YOUR TEAM?

A football team needs a quarterback, a center, linebackers, and other players working in harmony. No one player can win the game. All must be strong, fast, capable, and coordinated.

Your financial team needs at least some of the following players:

1. **CPA** addresses your tax, cash flow and debt/credit needs.

2. **Financial Planning Professional** addresses your wishes, dreams and goals, and develops a strategy for achieving them. They can charge a fee only, not charge a fee and receive sales commissions, or charge a fee and also receive commissions. The right planner or professional can act as your quarterback.

3. **Insurance Agent** addresses both business and personal insurance, as well as risk management planning.

4. **Wealth Manager** addresses risk, reward, and tax efficiencies of your investments.

5. **Pension Professional** addresses retirement issues and tax planning.

6. **Property, Casualty, Malpractice Professional** addresses your business insurance needs.

7. **Banker** addresses cash flow, lending and debt planning.

Picking winning players is essential. By understanding their important individual roles and making sure they all "join the huddle before the play," you increase your odds of success.

The seven advisors listed above fall into several financial categories: taxes, insurance, investments, and retirement. You probably won't need seven advisors on your team, but by understanding the differences between them and how they overlap, you'll be able to choose the resources that best fit your circumstances. The categories and advisor types are explored in detail in upcoming chapters.

HOW TO USE THIS BOOK

Think of this book as your personal financial guide. You'll start to work with trustworthy advisors to create a plan to help achieve financial security. Families can choose to bring this book to their trustworthy advisors. Trustworthy advisors can choose to share it with their clients and prospects to assist them in securing their financial health.

Each chapter contains information and questions to ask your advisor or yourself. Each chapter is organized into a practical and concise format so you can grasp the information quickly and discuss it with your own advisors.

Apply what you have learned, and let each chapter serve as a building block for the next. Focus on those chapters that are most appropriate and most immediate for you.

Being the financial advocate for your family is the financial journey of your lifetime, the kind that doesn't include directions, templates, warranties, or guarantees. This book provides tools which help to navigate your financial life calmly, accurately, and efficiently.

Plan each financial, investment and insurance project before you make financial decisions.

CHAPTER 2
TRUSTWORTHY ADVISORS

"When looking for people to invest with, always look for these three things: 1) Intelligence, 2) Energy and 3) Integrity. If number 3 doesn't exist, don't bother with the other two

—Warren Buffet

This chapter addresses the different types of advisors. A professional advisor should demonstrate trustworthiness. A trustworthy advisor gives you knowledge and confidence when making financial decisions. You'll have a plan and a process for managing that plan when you get off-track. Trust is very complex; developing trust is both a rational and an emotional process. Determining what team members you want in your financial life requires time and attention.

Trusting yourself first is the foundation for entering into a relationship with another person. If you don't, you may have a difficult time deciding whom to trust for financial, investment, and insurance advice. This book can help you make wiser financial decisions, but *you* will be the determining factor.

DIFFERENCES EXIST BETWEEN ADVISORS

According to the Investment Advisors Act of 1940, investment advisors are fiduciaries whose duty it is to seek to eliminate, or at least to expose, all potential conflicts of interest that might lead them to consciously or unconsciously give advice that is not in their client's best interest. A fiduciary advisor relationship usually applies legally to registered investment advisors.

For purposes of the book, a *fiduciary* advisor is an advisor who puts your interests ahead of his or her own, regardless of whether a regulatory authority requires transparency.

A *suitability* advisor is an advisor who provides a suitable product for your needs, but doesn't necessarily have to put your interests first. The Securities and Exchange Commission (SEC) defines "suitable" as being associated with a reasonable basis for the belief that a recommended transaction or investment plan involving a security or securities is a good fit for the client. The suitability standard generally applies to stockbrokers, registered representatives, and insurance agents.

A *fiduciary* "committed" investment or insurance advisor will sell you the *"right"* or most *"appropriate"* investment or insurance policy, not merely a *"suitable"* or *"good fit"* investment or insurance policy that may also pay them the highest compensation or reward.

In the financial services industry, there also are *transactional* salespeople. A *transactional* sales advisor might put the client first, but may be less skilled, product driven, and/or compensation driven.

Many advisors put their client's interest first, but a trusted team provides checks and balances against potential errors and conflicts. Fiduciary, suitability and transactional advisors can do a great, good, or unsatisfactory job for you. That is why you should create and qualify your own team of advisors.

TRUSTWORTHY ADVISORS

"Character" and "integrity" are not legal terms; they are human behavioral terms.

Trust is sacred. Trustworthy advisors differentiate themselves. They will usually tell you what you *need* to hear, not necessarily what you *want* to hear.

A trustworthy advisor is a *warrior* for you and your family. His or her job is to advise and assist you in doing the right things at the right time for the right reasons with the right people. They want you to have comprehensive advice, and give you information the way you need it.

INTEGRITY CONFLICTS

Conflicts of interest can arise in interactions with any advisor. As this book is being written, the US Department of Labor is addressing advisors' conflicts of interest. Warren Buffet said, "You can't see who is swimming naked until the tide goes out." Behind all communication and conversation is the question, "Can I trust you?"

An advisor conflict of interest might occur when one type of investment vehicle promises a different income stream to the advisor than another investment vehicle. Your advisor should recommend the right investment vehicle for you regardless of the revenue it brings to him. A trustworthy advisor will look at the relationship, not just the transaction, and will be less prone to potential conflicts of interest.

HOW CAN YOU TELL IF YOUR ADVISORS ARE THERE FOR YOU FIRST?

- They act with prudence, care, and good judgments at all times and are empathetic, confident, competent, and concise.

- They provide disclosure of potential conflicts, including additional incentive benefits a transaction may bring to them.

- They sit on "your side of the table" and see you as a long-term relationship, not just as a sale.

BUDDY TRUST

Choosing advisors is not about trusting your buddies, but about finding and working with competent professionals. Buddies are important to our personal and social networks. People are your buddies because you share something in common with them. You trust them as friends and confidants. You have a history with them and loyalty to that friendship.

The financial business of your family is a serious issue. It involves expertise and experience and possibly a different level of trust. A trustworthy advisor offers a true partnership where the advisor ties his/her own success to the success he/she brings to you.

You want an advisor who is both trustworthy and credible. You want an advisor who has the knowledge and the will to deliver on the promises you entrust to him. An advisor can build trust by being transparent and by showing you various ways to accomplish the same goal.

TRUST TENDENCIES

If you are a trusting person, you can be more susceptible to friend bias: *"Joe is my friend and would not do anything to hurt me."* The financial services industry knows this and promotes relationship selling as a result. Some people refer to this as *"blind trust."* Anybody can claim to be trustworthy. Trust carefully.

If you are a skeptical person, you may be hesitant to enter into a relationship. But once your decision is made, you may do everything you can to justify that trust. Many people want to prove to themselves, their loved ones, or their supervisors that they made the right decision. When confronted with the facts of what their buddy sold them, they often make excuses and stay with an inappropriate solution, in order to not offend their buddy.

SELF CONFIDENCE

Self-confidence comes from knowledge and/or experience in a particular area. Self-confidence can also come from setting and achieving goals. Sometimes egos get in the way when the *"financial patient"* wants to be the *"financial doctor."* Some doctors get angry when a patient comes into the office with the diagnosis and treatment already decided, just wanting an answer so they can leave. Some lawyers are the same way with their advisors. Overly confident lawyers sometimes don't accept sound recommendations because "they know better."

HOW TO EVALUATE ADVISORS

Salespeople can be hunters and you can be the prey. With all the financial services reform going on, there is no mandate for advisors to coordinate, collaborate, or communicate with your other advisors. The road of information can be paved with misinformation or incomplete information:

- In a buyer beware world, disclosures can be hard to read and hard to understand.

- In a buyer beware world, integrity can have three shades: black, white, and gray.

- In a buyer beware world, your advisor's check-book can influence how he or she treats *your* checkbook.

A trustworthy advisor should challenge your thinking. A trustworthy advisor should work with your other advisors in a spirit of cooperation, collaboration, and communication to spot things that can go wrong with your planning initiatives. Your team should proactively be part of the solution once a potential problem is identified.

CAN GOOGLE BE A TRUSTWORTHY ADVISOR?

Some lawyers trust Google and other lawyers more than they trust themselves and their advisors. They always have articles, commentaries, and opinions to share. They change their opinions often based on an article they read or the last conversation they had. The courthouse lobby is their investment-counseling center where lawyers become advisors to other lawyers and assist them in making financial decisions.

These lawyers have good intentions, and they seek out professional colleagues to support their opinions. They gather data and spend time planning. But they use their emotions to justify their decisions. They have a process they're comfortable with and they make the best decisions they can.

But when groups of clients discuss an article about legal findings, they usually lack the background to form well-founded opinions about the article's conclusions. Smart clients discuss these articles with their lawyers. Others become their own lawyer with possibly dangerous results.

Trusted advisors welcome your questions as an opportunity to help you understand the "big picture." And if the information you bring to the table is valid and valuable, a trustworthy advisor will consider how best to incorporate it into your ongoing plans without feeling upstaged.

CHARACTERISTICS OF
TRUSTWORTHY ADVISORS

- Trustworthy Advisors are clear about what they can and cannot help you with. They will recommend a subject matter expert if one is needed.

- A Trustworthy Advisor is authentic, a thought leader, and proactive. He or she understands your risk tolerance and your "end game."

- Trustworthy Advisors offers solutions you can't come up with on your own and provide a succinct, polished recommendation outlining what you need to know or do to make an informed decision.

EFFECTIVE LISTENING IS CRITICAL TO BEING A TRUSTWORTHY ADVISOR

It is very important that you work with committed listeners. The following will not be easy to see unless you are a committed listener and are listening for these types of advisors.

"Committed" listeners listen empathetically, from your perspective.

"Selective" listeners listen for selling opportunities. They are sometimes listening for your pain so they can alleviate it with a product sale. Selective listeners can listen as advisors, but not as well as "committed" listeners.

"Pretend" listeners listen only to let you finish what you want to say so they can go straight into their sales presentation. Ask yourself: is my advisor really listening to me?

Selling is a process of convincing someone to buy something. *Advising* is a process of identifying a need and coming up with the best solution to fulfill that need.

A trustworthy advisor was introduced to a lawyer in his late 30s. They started speaking about risk management. The lawyer had a wife and three young children. He kept telling the advisor he didn't need more life insurance. The more they spoke, the more they both realized that what he didn't need was more insurance *premium*. He definitely needed more life insurance and other agents had tried to sell him more, but other agents had tried to sell him policies that accumulate cash value; they were good policies but he could not afford them now.

Once they agreed on his needs, timeline, and budget, they were able to create a term policy solution that would take him to retirement and provide sufficient income to his family if he did not make it to retirement. They protected his family by moving beyond buying and selling to *advising*.

FINANCIAL INTERACTIONS
OR SIDE EFFECTS

A pharmacist is trained to understand the interactions of combinations of chemicals. When my father-in-law was in his 80s, his hands started shaking. We took him to his doctor, who told us that he had Parkinson's disease and there was nothing we could do about it.

My friend Arthur, who is a pharmacist, said, "Give me a list of his medications." He got back to me and said that a particular medication my father-in-law was on had Parkinson's-like symptoms as a potential side effect. He said, "take him off of that medication for one week to see if he stops shaking"

After three days off this medicine, my father-in-law stopped shaking. He passed away at the age of 92 and never developed Parkinson's disease. In a "financial pharmacy" environment, certain combinations of financial products can create conflicts that can partially offset the intended benefits.

Your trusted team should be able to evaluate your financial products for conflicts and overlaps.

PROFESSIONAL QUALIFICATIONS

We think of advisors as professionals in a particular field. Research a prospective advisor's title or professional certification if you are relying on those certifications for advice. Ask your advisor to explain what he or she did to qualify for that title. For example: "I had to complete 60 hours of coursework and sit for a series of comprehensive exams."

Partial list of titles and designations found in the financial services industry:

Wealth Manager
Insurance Agent
Financial Planner
Financial Advisor
Financial Consultant
Retirement Professional
Investment Manager
Investment Consultant
Investment Advisor Representative

Designations include:

Certified Financial Planner (CFP®)
Certified Funds Specialist (CFS)
Chartered Life Underwriter (CLU®)
Chartered Financial Consultant (ChFC®)
Chartered Advisor in Philanthropy (CAP)
Accredited Domestic Partnership Advisor (ADPA)

When it comes to choosing trustworthy advisors, designations and titles can show a certain level of certification or accomplishment. A designation or title, however, is no guarantee of professionalism or that a particular advisor is the right fit for your particular needs.

11 QUESTIONS TO ASK YOURSELF ABOUT PROSPECTIVE ADVISORS

If you answer "no" to any of the following questions, reconsider your prospective advisor carefully before you proceed.

1. Does this advisor inspire confidence? If not, why?

2. Is this advisor knowledgeable and skillful?

3. Does this advisor's body language, conversation, and tone of voice make you feel safe?

4. Is this advisor respectful of your concerns and of you?

5. Is this advisor willing to educate you so you can make informed decisions?

6. Does this advisor have a true problem-solving attitude or is he or she just trying to sell you something?

7. Will this advisor continue to educate you as markets and financial solution changes occur?

8. Does this advisor really listen to you or is he more focused on what he wants to say?

9. Does this advisor challenge you or just take purchase orders?

10. Will this advisor be proactive in calling you when there are changes you should know about?

11. Is this the advisor you want to entrust with your assets? *If no, consider this a deal killer.*

11 QUESTIONS TO ASK
YOUR ADVISORS ABOUT THEMSELVES

These questions can offer an opportunity to get to know an advisor, and what you can expect from them:

1. What are your core competencies and where are you most experienced and knowledgeable?

2. What makes you unique in your marketplace?

3. What other knowledge do you have?

4. How often will we speak?

5. How often will I receive statements? Will they come from you or from a third party?

6. If I purchase a product from you, how many options will you show me? Will you review the pros and cons of your recommendations? How will you make me comfortable that I am making the right decision?

7. If you ask me to make a financial or an insurance decision based on an illustration, will you explain the illustration to me?

8. Will you explain to me how my insurance policy is performing, after I purchase it?

9. How often should we meet to review how I am doing?

10. How will you be compensated?

11. Will you work with other members of my team? *If no, consider this a deal killer.*

CHAPTER 3
FINANCIAL PLAQUE

Your dentist defines plaque as a sticky film of bacteria that forms on your teeth. If left untreated, plaque can lead to tooth and gum disease.

In the neurological world, protein fragments can destroy synapses where nerve cells relay signals to each other. This buildup of brain plaque can lead to memory loss and other brain illnesses.

In the cardiovascular world, plaque is a buildup of fatty substance in the arteries that can develop into coronary heart disease.

Financial plaque is a buildup of poor financial decisions made over a period of time. The impact usually does not show up for many years or until a life-changing event occurs and can have a negative or even catastrophic financial impact on you and/ or your family.

Seven guiding principles govern the management of your finances and help you avoid financial plaque.

Your advisors' roles are to create awareness, deliver guidance and coaching, and mentor you through the stages of financial management and protection. Keep your financial smile bright, your financial brain sharp, and your financial arteries flowing freely by making wise financial choices.

7 GUIDING PRINCIPLES THAT PROTECT YOU AGAINST FINANCIAL PLAQUE

1. **You will always care more about protecting your family than any advisor will.** Outsourcing your family's financial advocacy to anyone other than your spouse or a trustworthy advisor could be considered family malpractice. Put a planning process in place with the right advisors behind you. Do the little things right: Write a will. Make a plan. Protect yourself from catastrophic risk. Build a foundation for financial success. As the one who cares most, monitor your own financial health, research advisors' recommendations, monitor progress, and ask questions. Your team works for *you*.

2. **You will always have to be the decision maker of your financial team.** The right team culture

can produce the right results. The wrong team culture can result in mistakes that may ruin your strategy. Poor family governance, incompatible business partners, advisors' conflicting compensation models, and conflicts of interest can damage or destroy your financial health. As team leader, *you* are responsible for communication. Establish and enforce a communication schedule for your team members that connect them both to each other and to you. Don't assume they will collaborate regularly without your leadership.

3. **Your Purpose, Vision, Values (PVV).** It is easy to deviate from your plan. Toys, rewards, vacations, and "best thing since sliced bread" investments will come your way in abundance.

- **Purpose:** Create peace of mind and financial freedom for you and your family by having clear financial goals.

- **Vision:** Combine your purpose and your values into a powerful planning and action process to solve problems with your team of trusted advisors.

- **Values:** Always be trustworthy in your commitments so your financial goals happen.

4. **Do more with less.** Financial pressures mandate efficiency and effectiveness. Being efficient and effective with your money when purchasing financial products and services is critical. You don't necessarily need more advisors, more diversification, and more risk. What you need is advisors you can trust. It's not the *quantity* but the *quality* of advisors that creates powerful results. The right team creates efficiencies and effectiveness in managing your finances.

5. **Understand potential financial cliffs.** Understanding whom you work for, what control you have over your career, and what control you have over your income is essential. Will your income be fixed as a salary, variable based on originations and work performed, or a combination? What employee benefits do you need to protect you and your family? Who pays for these benefits? How will you monitor all the things you need to keep track of financially, and who can help you? What is your exit strategy if things

don't work as planned, and how do you prepare for it?

6. **Pay yourself first.** Your strategy may not work out as planned. Invest in yourself first. Everything and everyone else comes second. Paying off current debt, paying for important insurance, and saving for a down payment on a house, are examples of paying yourself first. Always include an emergency reserve in your working capital plan. Your team should work together to develop a safe financial cushion for you. Start with safe money planning before you attempt speculative or unpredictable money planning. Debt and loss create negative financial leverage and moves you further away from your financial freedom.

7. **Time can be your best friend and your worst enemy.** Time can cost you money if you wait too long to save and invest; time can make you money if you start early and remain focused. Time is the one thing you can never get back. Compound interest is about making money on your money over time. Stock market results are about your time horizon in the market, not

about timing the market by shuffling in and out of investments.

7 USEFUL SECOND OPINIONS

1. **Disability Insurance policy second opinion.** All disability companies and policies are not alike. An attorney who worked for a law firm had a group disability policy that would pay him $5,000 a month if he became disabled. He also purchased an individual policy from his insurance agent that would pay $5,000 a month. An insurance review of his group policy indicated that the group policy had an offset provision. An offset provision allows the insurance company to account for your other coverage and pay you only the difference between the two. If the attorney had gone out on a disability claim, he would have had to decide whom to file the claim with.

   Even though he was paying for $10,000 a month of total coverage, if he filed a claim with his individual carrier for $5,000 a month worth of benefit, his group carrier would not pay the claim.

2. **Life Insurance policy second opinion.** An attorney had a very old whole life policy that he had

properly funded for many years. The contract required that he fund it for his entire life. He was getting ready to retire and also had a loan on the policy; he wanted to stop making payments when he stopped working. A life insurance diagnostic audit revealed several other insurance company contracts that were more flexible in premium payments, had lower costs of insurance, and lower premiums. By applying for a new policy with another company, he was able to use the cash value of the existing policy to pay for the new one without making any more premium payments. He had been happy and complacent with his life insurance policy before the review because he was unaware of available options.

3. **Long-term Care Insurance policy second opinion.** When purchasing long-term care insurance, consider inflation. A diagnostic long-term care insurance audit revealed that when a lawyer had purchased a policy many years before, an appropriate amount of coverage was $150 a day. Today, many advisors suggest $250 a day. The audit determined that the existing policy was still fine and appropriate, and the attorney determined that he did not want to self-insure the

extra $100 a day. He bought a second policy for $100 a day, bringing the total to $250 a day of coverage in case he needed this care in the future. The coverage he originally purchased was probably sufficient, but his personal financial needs and rising costs of living required him to purchase additional insurance.

4. **Retirement Investment plan second opinion.** Retirement planning is a special and tricky endeavor. Work with professionals who are well versed in pension and tax law issues. As practice owners, lawyers can take on the role of retirement plan fiduciary and the responsibility/liability for compliance of the plan. Uninformed business owners can potentially violate fiduciary rules they have as the plan sponsor and/or administrator. Some plans are federally sponsored plans and some are state sponsored plans; make sure you know the difference. If you have employees and assume fiduciary responsibility for their retirement plan, make sure you have professionals guiding you.

5. **Non-Retirement Investment plan second opinion.** Many life insurance policy reviews indicate that a policy could collapse from underfunding

or underperformance or a combination of both. A review should be completed *every year* to see if you are on or off-track, just like your annual physical examination determines the status of your health. Your life insurance policy should not be filed away forever and never reviewed. Industry underwriting and products change, and you may miss opportunities to improve your policy coverage and/or pricing.

6. **Tax Strategies second opinion.** Tax deductions are usually granted for money you put into a retirement plan. Generally, you will pay tax on everything you take out. You will only be able to spend the dollars you take home *after* the taxes are paid, so have a diagnostic audit performed by someone who understands your needs and the various tax strategies available. Involve your accountant, your insurance advisor, and your investment professionals working together.

7. **Legal Documents second opinion.** Legal documents, such as wills and trusts, can become outdated. When you die, unless your paperwork is kept current, your estate will be distributed according to your legal documents, not accord-

ing to your intentions. Many families fight over inheritances and possessions because there were no clear legal documents in place.

4 CRITICAL REVIEWS THAT CAN PREVENT OR REVERSE FINANCIAL PLAQUE

1. Legal Documents Review

Meet with a tax and estate-planning attorney to determine what documents you need to have in place. Find these documents and review them periodically. When one attorney's children were small, he set up his best friends as his trustees, there to raise his children if he and his wife were no longer alive. Then the friends got divorced and he had his parents placed in that role. Then his mother died so he changed the trustee role to his brother. Had he not updated his documents, if he and his spouse had died unexpectedly, his children could have been stuck in a l egal quagmire.

2. Asset Protection Planning Review

Meet with an advisor and an asset protection attorney who understand asset protection laws in the specific state where you practice. Titling of assets is critical to properly protecting them.

Incomplete titling by attorneys who think they are asset protected often creates exposure to malpractice creditors.

3. Risk Management Review

Meet with an insurance professional or a financial planner to determine your financial needs. Factor in the length of time you will need each type of insurance coverage and the options available, while gauging your budget considerations. There are so many solutions to insurance protection; it is difficult to evaluate and compare them without professional guidance.

4. Income Tax Review

Meet with your tax advisor to determine the tax efficiencies of each of your investments. If you have ever complained to your accountant that you are paying too much income tax, a line-by-line analysis of your tax return will reveal exactly where your tax money is going.

10 COMMON MISTAKES
MADE IN FINANCIAL PLANNING

1. Failure to recognize that your financial plan should be treated like a potential chronic illness.

2. Failure to recognize that if there is no plan, then that *is* your plan.

3. Failure to recognize the rule of "diagnosis before prescription" says that you should not purchase a financial service or product until you are clear about how it will integrate with all of your other products, and help you achieve your strategic financial goals.

4. Failure to recognize that a potential chronic financial condition should be monitored on a regular basis.

5. Failure to recognize that being busy is not an excuse for not protecting your family.

6. Failure to build a team of advisors and who work together.

7. Failure to recognize that retirement, college, graduate school, and weddings may be an 18–35-year financial commitment, which needs to be managed throughout its duration.

8. Failure to recognize predatory advisors who put their interests above yours.

9. Failure to recognize that any insurance that is subject to medical underwriting should be bought before you can't medically qualify for it.

10. Failure to recognize that if you don't pay your-self first, your lifestyle may eat up your income and your savings.

CHAPTER 4
KEY CORNERSTONES
OF PLANNING

"Life is what happens to you while you are busy making other plans."

—John Lennon

The key cornerstones of planning are:

- **Identifying** risk.

- **Developing** a strategy to manage and mitigate that risk.

- **Implementing** solutions to manage and mitigate that risk.

- **Monitoring** results and breakdowns, and taking actions to correct those breakdowns.

The foundation of a great plan starts with:

"How would I live my life if money was not a concern?"

The major components of planning are: discovery of your current financial situation and concerns, gathering financial and non-financial information, establishing priorities, and creating a strategy and action plan. Your advisors can suggest goals and assist you with managing those goals.

WHEN PLANNING WORKS AND WHEN IT DOESN'T!

Planning is not about the destination, but about the journey. The journey requires a collaborative planning process involving you and your trusted advisors. Without a plan, you won't know what your problems are and how to solve them. Without a meaningful plan, you may work on the wrong projects or move in the wrong direction, losing precious time and resources. Take responsibility for understanding and approving the plan so it becomes *your* plan and not your advisors'.

The question to ask your team is, "How will this planning process lead me to achieve my goals?"

OWNERSHIP OF YOUR PLAN IS KEY

A financial plan is a snapshot of your current financial situation. It's a compilation of the information you give your advisor, the information your advisor decides to put in the plan, and how the specific software generates the information you will review together.

In 1956, Herbert Simon, a Nobel Prize-winning economist, sociologist, and psychologist, combined the words "satisfy" and "suffice" to explain the behavior of decision-makers who couldn't find an optimal solution. Even without an optimal solution, some attorneys will come up with a solution or resolution and make a decision just to get the process over with. Without a plan and a planner, many attorneys are prone to "satisfice."

Satisfice is a capitulation, where you give up your resistance to making a decision, and make the best decision you can make at that moment, so you can move on and put the agony of the decision-making process behind you. This is "default planning." Default planning occurs when decisions are made for you, because you don't make them *yourself.*

Planning can be difficult and time-consuming. It requires you to gather information, learn new concepts, place your trust in third parties, and weigh options you may not feel qualified to consider. But with your financial health at stake, engagement with the planning process is critical. Good advisors can make your planning journey easier and even pleasant.

WEALTHY LAWYER VS. LESS PROSPEROUS LAWYER WHAT'S THE DIFFERENCE IN THEIR THINKING?

Smart planning is about mitigating risk. Smart planning addresses risk in proportion equal to reward. Wealthy lawyers expect the best and prepare for the worst, and usually make fewer financial mistakes than less prosperous ones. Wealthy lawyers understand the difference between immediate and delayed gratification. Why is it that some lawyers can make millions of dollars over the course of their professional careers and still not be able to retire comfortably, while some lawyers make much less and retire in comfort? A younger lawyer once asked his boss, "How do I become a millionaire?" His boss said immediately, "That's easy. Make two million dollars and only lose a million."

In medicine, physicians use SOAP (Subjective, Objective, Assessment, and Plan) notes to document and communicate information with peers and patients. Use this same process to manage your financial and family life.

1. **Create** inspiring goals or objectives.

2. **Formulate** specific strategies for achieving them.

3. **Arrange** or create the means required.

4. **Implement,** direct, and monitor all steps in the proper order.

EXECUTION RISK

Execution risk is another way to look at errors and mistakes. Even if a plan is followed to the letter, the results may not work out as planned. Vague goals can be too easy to achieve without producing a meaningful result. Goals should be as well defined as possible. A goal of, "I want to lose 10 pounds in the next 30 days" is more meaningful and measurable than "I want to lose weight." The more specific and detailed a goal is, the better prepared you'll be to manage execution risk.

BRICOLAGE PLANNING

Bricolage is a French word for "tinkering." *Bricolage* is construction from whatever materials are at hand. Many lawyers have semi-plans, partial plans, several plans, plans in process, and plans created at different times with different people. They are collectors of financial products that, like medications, may create side effects and duplication.

Create an organizational structure with your advisors to determine how the roles, responsibilities, and decision-making will be assigned, controlled, and coordinated. Determine how information flows from team member to team member.

CREATE YOUR PROBLEM SOLVING VISION AS A STARTING POINT.

Building a team culture of accountability is a critical component of working together. Get trustworthy advisors on your team who work toward a common goal. In an accountable financial care structure, your trustworthy advisors team creates balance and offers useful advice.

TYPES OF PLANS AND ANALYSES

"Plan for the future because that's where you are going to spend the rest of your life."

—Mark Twain

Be clear about what a plan really is.

- A **Financial Plan** can determine and guide in managing your finances over time in a way that helps meet your family's needs. A Financial Plan involves data, discovery, and metrics.

- A **Life Plan** can clarify your dreams, goals, and legacy, what you want to accomplish, how you want to live, and what's important to you so you can establish a work/life balance that will make you happy. A Life Plan involves feelings and emotions.

- A **Strategic Plan** is an action plan that can determine and manages what your goals are, and how you want to achieve them. A Strategic Plan involves data, metrics, emotions, and feelings.

- A **Needs Analysis** can determine how much money your family will need after you die. A needs analysis is included in a financial plan.

- A **Financial Analysis** is an income and expense statement showing how much money you keep after taxes and where it is being spent, saved, or squandered. A financial analysis is included in your plan.

- A **Retirement Analysis** can determine how much income you will need in retirement assuming retirement at a specific age, living to your life expectancy, your lifestyle, and the projected rate of inflation. This analysis is also included in your financial plan.

- An **Estate Plan** spells out your wishes after you die. These legal documents memorialize your intentions and required actions.

- A financial plan can also be a family plan. A financial plan is only valuable if it includes deliverables, a timeline, and you follow them.

DEBT

Managing debt is an important foundation for financial planning. Some advisors classify debt as positive and negative. As an example, if you can borrow money at 4% and make 8% with that money, some advisors consider that positive debt. But unless the 8% is guaranteed or highly predictable, this strategy is risky.

Eliminate debt with a budget. A budget is like a collection of labeled jars that hold expenses. Since you only have so much money to put into your jars, you are in control of determining how much money goes into each. If you don't monitor them, the bigger jars will catch more of your money and you may lose control over your budget.

Debt can be a stressful and demotivating influence. Set goals for yourself and reward yourself for each success. Your goal might be to pay off all your debt, including auto, home and consumer loans.

CREDIT CARDS

Debt can impact your FICO credit score: A FICO score is the credit score most lenders use to determine your credit risk. The score ranges from a low of 300 to a high of 850. The higher the score, the lower the interest rates you can qualify for when you buy homes or cars, or apply for credit cards. This score considers your payment history, whether you've made credit payments on time, the total amount of debt you owe, the length of time of your credit history, any new credit you have, and the types of credit you have used in the past.

Part of your FICO credit score is called a "credit utilization ratio." It is the sum of the balances on all your credit cards divided by the total credit limit on all your cards. It's good to keep this ratio under 30%. For example, if you have two cards with $25,000 credit limits, the total limit is $50,000. Therefore $50,000 x 30% ratio equals $15,000. To keep this ratio intact, try to keep your unpaid credit card balances under $15,000 if you are applying for a home mortgage or other credit.

If you have too many cards, do not cancel them. Cut them up. Canceling them may increase your credit utilization ratio and decrease your FICO score. Debt is a piece of a financial picture.

SUMMARY POINTS TO
HELP YOU WITH YOUR CREDIT

Always pay at least the minimum payment required before the due date. If you can pay your entire monthly balance off each month, do it.

- Once you have a card, don't close it. Build credit by having open credit. Use these cards once in a while and pay your entire bill in the month it is due.

- If you plan to buy a home soon, don't open up any new credit. Every time you apply for credit, except for mortgages, your credit score goes down a couple of points. Review your credit report at least annually and dispute any information that is not correct.

FreeCreditReport.com and Quizzle.com offer copies of your credit report. For more information about your credit score, go to www.myfico.com

SECTION TWO SUMMARY: RISK

Risk is the probability or threat of damage, injury, liability, loss, or any other unwanted occurrence caused by external or internal forces, that may be addressed through preventative action. We purchase insurance to protect against the things we fear. Any time you can mitigate risk with a check, you've made a wise investment.

> *Insure everything you cannot afford to lose and self-insure everything else.*

We will all experience volatile and unpredictable economic climates. It is more important than ever to make sure your business and personal assets are properly protected.

We know we can't eliminate risk, but we can prepare for and manage it.

Understand the different types of risk, tradeoffs regarding risk, and how to put a price tag on each risk. Your advisory team's role is to create a cost/benefit analysis of each potential risk.

There are two risk categories:

High cost/low probability risks aren't likely to happen, but could be devastating if they do occur. Examples are hurricanes and earthquakes.

Low cost/high probability risks are likely to occur, but will probably not be devastating if they do, such as a sickness requiring a doctor visit or a short-term disability.

Risk management strategy: Determine if you can convert a serious financial risk into a manageable ongoing premium.

People often buy insurance if they have experienced loss or damage personally or watched another person experience it. Risk management insurance will probably be your largest single expense. It covers dying too soon, living too long, living with a disability, getting sued, losing something valuable, and income tax leakage.

Which risk management mistake will have the

most impact on you and your family? After all, the purpose of risk management is to prevent an accident from wrecking your life.

Identify the right strategies and solutions to effectively manage the various risks that arise at all phases of life. Risk management is a sign of maturity, boldness, conviction, bravery, and love for family. One catastrophic event can destroy a lifetime of planning. Being able to afford risk and choosing to take on risk are very different considerations.

If you do not have a mortgage on your home, no lender requires you to purchase homeowner's, hurricane, and flood insurance. You can choose to self-insure. Do you want to save the premium and absorb the potential risk of not having coverage, or do you want to pay the premium and not have to worry? Risk management is the trading of a small, known loss (premiums) to avoid a bigger, unknown loss (severe damage or destruction).

There are many risks in life; how many do you want to self-insure? Balance premiums against the cost of catastrophic damage. Allocate and budget premium dollars to mitigate these risks. Reposition premium dollars as your risks increase and decrease over time.

SELF-INSURED, PARTIALLY INSURED, FULLY-INSURED: YOU DECIDE

In a self-insured situation, you have no insurance. You are prepared to absorb all risks as they occur and will fund that loss with your personal dollars. When self-insuring, the cost of being wrong usually exceeds the cost of being right.

In a fully insured situation, you have insurance protection for every risk.

In a partially insured situation, you choose what you want and don't want to insure. You control your risk by determining how much risk you will keep and how much you will transfer to the insurance company.

Insurance protection comes from different companies offering policies with different designs, definitions, tradeoffs, and strengths. Address risk by determining how much coverage you need, how long you want coverage for, what you want to accomplish, and what happens if you want to extend the term of coverage.

TYPES OF RISK

Risky behavior and predatory advisors: Risky behavior is when your safe money becomes your play money. Credit card debt buildup, gambling, addictions, and impulsive buying can derail financial management planning.

Family health issues and premature death: Unexpected health issues can affect a family physically, financially and emotionally. Assuming that you will always be able to work and to continue to earn your income has risk.

The three I's. Inflation, Interest Rates and Income Taxes: Which way do you think they are going? Unmanaged money can decrease in value, another risk factor.

Allocation Risk/Location Risk/Sequence of Returns Risk: Allocation risk is about types of investments, such as stocks, bonds, and cash. Location risk is about the tax impact on your different investments. Sequence of Returns risk is about the financial impact of market volatility on your investments.

Divorce: Preparing with and dealing with divorce can include nuptial agreements:

These agreements address individual property and marital property, asset protection, malpractice protection, asset conservation, division of qualified retirement plans, debt liability and responsibilities for existing and future debt, and community property agreements if you are located in a community property state.

Address these potential risks with your trust worthy advisory team.

TYPES OF INSURANCE
RISK MANAGEMENT TOOLS

Disability Insurance can help protect you if become disabled and can't work.

- Group: Offered by employers and usually paid for by the employer.

- Individual: Purchased on your own.

Life Insurance can help protect your family if you pass away.

- Group: Offered by employers and usually paid for by the employer.

- Individual: Purchased on your own.

Long-term Care Insurance can help protect you and your family if you can't take care of yourself.

- Group: Offered by employers and can be employer or employee paid.

- Individual: Purchased on your own.

Homeowner's and Auto Insurance can help protect you if you experience a financial loss on your house or automobile.

- Individual: Some companies will offer you a discount if you purchase both policies with them.

Umbrella Insurance can help protect your assets from claims that are greater than your homeowner's and automobile liability coverage, up to the limits you purchased on your umbrella policy. They can protect your home, rental property, and automobiles from financial risks up to your coverage amount.

CHAPTER 5
LIFE INSURANCE

"People who die without life insurance should have
to come back and clean up the mess they left behind."
—Mark Twain

Think about what insurance *does,* not about what it *is.* What it does is help protect your downside from a catastrophic, unforeseen risk.

Think of life insurance as a long-term investment made by you on behalf of your family. You won't ever see a return if you invest wisely, but your family will.

This chapter explores the types of life insurance policies, how they work, and how to understand the information presented to you by an insurance agent. Your advisor's role is to help you identify your insurable needs, present you with viable insurance options, and explain the pros and cons of each option.

The right advisor helps you secure the right amount of coverage at the right time for the right price. Every insurance policy you own is an asset.

If you own health, dental, vision, or hospitalization insurance, these assets help protect your net worth if you require medical care. If you own auto, property, or casualty insurance, these assets help protect your net worth if you have an accident or catastrophe.

Life Insurance can serve several purposes:

- It can create income replacement to a beneficiary upon death of the insured; it can complete educational savings for the children and it can complete a retirement savings plan for the surviving spouse.

- It can create business continuation protection if an owner or partner dies and it can pay off debt, taking financial pressure off your family and/or business.

- It can create estate preservation protection to pay estate and inheritance taxes.

- It can create estate and business equalization so specific assets can go to specific people.

Three ingredients underlie the decision to purchase life insurance:

- Someone you love would be financially impacted by your death.

- You are medically and financially qualified and approved.

- You can afford to fund the solution to the above problem by paying insurance premiums.

THE PARTIES IN A
LIFE INSURANCE CONTRACT

The parties in a life insurance contract are the *insured,* the *owner,* and the *beneficiary.* The insured is the person whose life is covered. The owner controls the contract and is the only person or entity allowed to receive information about the policy. The beneficiary is the person or entity that receives the proceeds from the insurance policy when the insured dies. The owner has control of who receives the insurance proceeds, and controls and owns any cash accumulation inside the policy.

DON'T WAIT TO BUY LIFE INSURANCE

Most life insurance is priced based on your *attained* age, not your actual age. When you are six months plus one day past your birthday, your premium cost is based on your attained age, the age you'll be on your *next* birthday. By waiting to buy life insurance, you pay more and you risk deterioration of your health due to accidents or aging. The less healthy you are, the more insurance will cost you, or you may become uninsurable and unable to obtain any life insurance.

HEALTH AND FINANCIAL UNDERWRITING

Medical underwriting has become very sophisticated. If you have one health issue, underwriting can be very straightforward. If you have multiple health issues, underwriting can become more complicated. Insurance companies intentionally focus on age, gender, and health to compete for your business.

A husband who is healthy, but a smoker, and a wife who is a less healthy but a non-smoker, may end up insured by different companies because of the underwriting considerations for their different health classifications.

Health and financial underwriting is based on your personal economic value and the needs of your family. Life insurance companies will generally underwrite up to 20 to 30 times your annual income. If more coverage is needed, a letter will be required to explain your need for additional coverage.

PERMANENTLY OWNING VS. TEMPORARILY RENTING LIFE INSURANCE

Historically, the insurance industry has referred to term insurance as "renting insurance" and all cash value insurance policies as "owning insurance." Due to the variables and assumptions of cash value life insurance, it's not that simple. Cash value policies, which are usually sold to last "forever," may not last forever or even long enough to pay a claim. Factors that can negatively impact life insurance include: not designing the policy correctly, and not funding it properly or on time. Your projected dividend, interest rate, or rate of return will probably not consistently perform as illustrated. Therefore your projected result may not be realized as planned.

POLICY RIDERS

Riders are policy enhancements that come at a cost. You may not need any riders. Your trusted advisors will analyze the costs/benefits of riders and assist you in making decisions about what riders are valuable to you. Some examples of life insurance riders are: waiver of the premium for the cost of insurance in the event of permanent disability, long-term care rider to cover chronic care expenses, and a return of premium rider on term policies that pays if you live past the expiration of the term period.

POTENTIAL TAX IMPLICATIONS OF LIFE INSURANCE

Life insurance proceeds can be income tax-free to the beneficiaries named in the policy. It is also possible to access policy gains tax-free providing it is not a modified endowment contract (MEC).[1] Make sure your insurance agent explains the difference between taking out the premiums you paid in as a *distribution,* and taking out the gains you accumulated as a *loan,* and how these impact your policy. Understand the interest charges on loans, where they come from, and how these loans and interest impact your policy.

Why do so many people purchase life insurance that terminates before they do? You can't know what your insurance needs will be 10, 20, 30 and 40 years from now. That's why insurance planning is critical every year, just like an annual health checkup. Life insurance becomes life *assurance,* one day after you pass away with a life insurance policy still in place.

LIFE INSURANCE AS A FINANCIAL *ASSET*

Many people do not own appropriate life insurance because they are not clear about their goals and the purpose of owning life insurance. The greatest strength of life insurance is its ability to pay a specific amount of money upon the death of the insured. Depending on when death occurs, your beneficiaries can potentially receive a large death benefit relative to the amount of premiums paid.

Some professionals think of life insurance only as a way to provide for a surviving family. But wealthy families can use life insurance as an asset to create wealth. By reserving a portion of your assets each year to cover the cost of life insurance premiums, you may be able to transfer additional wealth to your family upon your death.

The death benefit offered by life insurance provides another opportunity: Because the financial risk of dying is shifted from your other assets to the life insurance carrier, you may be able to protect a portion of your financial assets against fluctuations in the marketplace. Knowing that your beneficiaries will be cared for will also free you to make additional choices with your remaining investments.

A comprehensive plan that includes life insurance offers the opportunity to leverage your investment strategy to help maximize returns and minimize risk. The cash surrender value of your life insurance policies are a part of your net worth; a safety net that can allow you to invest your other monies without potentially putting your family at additional risk.

Cash value life insurance policies can be considered a financial asset because they can grow in value based on the type of policy. Cash value life insurance policies allow for premium payment amounts above the cost of insurance to collect in a cash value account. It is important to understand how your cash value grows with each insurance company and for each type of policy.

Buy life insurance as an asset when it can become a valuable piece of your diversified portfolio, creating tax deferred buildup of your cash value.[2] You can increase your cash value by making additional premiums subject to IRS guidelines.

Regardless of the provider or type of policy, prior or current returns are not a predictor of future returns. Unless a policy is guaranteed to continue to a certain age regardless of policy fees, expenses and returns, it may not continue as planned. Work with an advisor who will help you understand your policy, and review your insurance assets at least annually.

THERE ARE BASICALLY
SEVEN TYPES OF LIFE INSURANCE.

Review your life insurance policies to see which types of life insurance you have. Each insurance company has versions of these types of policies with marketing names attached to them. Side-by-side comparisons of both term and cash value policies are very difficult, due to the many assumptions and variations between contracts. Relying on a knowledgeable and experienced insurance professional will help you make the right decision for your particular need.

1   **Level Term Insurance** is designed to provide pure protection only, designed to protect your loved ones for a specific period of time. Term insurance has no cash value buildup. Term insurance has a fixed death benefit for the life of the policy, but the premium you pay is only fixed for a specific period of time, usually 10, 15, 20, 25, or 30 years. After the fixed period of time is over, your policy will continue, but your premium will increase significantly. You set the timeline for the premium when you purchase the policy.

2   **Traditional Whole Life Insurance** is designed to protect your loved ones as long as you fund the policy correctly. When you die, your family gets the death benefit and the insurance company usually gets the cash buildup accumulated in the policy. The cash value of the policy is designed to keep your premiums level; it goes to the insurance company when you pass away. Whole life insurance has a fixed premium you must pay to qualify for the declared guarantees in the contract. The growth of the cash value is based on declared dividends and paid up additions. Whole life policies offer either a fixed or an increasing death benefit.

3   **Universal Life Insurance** offers flexible premiums and cash value build up. This type of policy is designed so you control how long the policy continues. It offers a flexible or a fixed death benefit, depending on the amount and timing of the payments. Unlike Whole Life insurance, Universal Life Insurance allows you to use the interest from the accumulated cash value to help pay the premium. Growth of the cash value is based on the interest rate on each policy anniversary date.

4 **Indexed Universal Life Insurance** fits in between a universal life policy and a variable life insurance policy. Even though this type of policy is called "indexed," the cash value is not invested in index funds. The growth of the cash value is an interest-crediting factor based on specific index-linked crediting or interest rates as outlined in your specific policy.

The product is designed to provide upside potential with maximum caps and protection against market downturns. Usually, the floor of your index is zero and your cap may be 8%. That means no matter what happens with your index return; you will never receive less than zero percent return or greater than 8% in that same period. Indexed life policies offer a flexible death benefit with flexible premiums.

This is a complex product with assumptions based on historical returns of the index presented to you. All indexed life policies have different costs and different index crediting assumptions.

5 **Variable Universal Life Insurance** is specifically designed to be overfunded as much as possible up to Internal Revenue Service (IRS)

limits, where part of the premiums goes to pay the cost of the insurance and other charges, and the remainder goes into investments you choose. This is the only life insurance product that offers true investments. This is the only life insurance product registered with the SEC (Securities and Exchange Commission).[3]

Many companies offer over 50 different fund options covering all asset classes, including asset allocation funds, where a team of managers is in charge of allocating your investments based on your risk profile. Investment dollars can be transferred from one investment to another without incurring fees or income taxes. Variable universal life offers flexible or fixed death benefits with flexible premiums. The cash value can grow or decline based on the performance of the market-based investment options you choose.

Don't plan on buying this type of policy and putting it in a drawer forever. Investments need to be reviewed periodically. Track how they are performing. These investments are held in separate accounts from the insurance companies' general accounts. The policy owner bears all investment risk associated with the underlying funds.

6   **Institutional Grade Life Insurance** is a cash value policy. It can be corporately or individually owned. It can be a whole life, universal life, indexed life or variable life product. What makes this type of insurance unique is that it has no surrender charges, like traditional cash value life insurance. Traditional life insurance is designed to be funded with the least amount of premium to accomplish your goals. The benefit arises in institutional grade life insurance when the cash value of the policy becomes larger than the premiums paid. Plans utilizing these type policies generally are designed to fund the policies up to the IRS's legal tax limits. Your qualified insurance advisor will design this policy in accordance with IRS statute 7702A of the Internal Revenue Code.

7   **Survivorship or Second-to-Die Life Insurance** is a type of life insurance policy based on the lives of two people. It can be purchased to pay estate taxes and buy out businesses partners. It can be purchased even if one spouse is uninsurable. Often less expensive than two separate individual policies, this type of insurance is usually restricted to married couples. It pays proceeds only after the second partner's death.

How do you evaluate these different types of life insurance policies? All insurance policies have "illustrations" or proposals that explain their details. Cash value illustrations present many assumptions and are often difficult to understand. Ask your insurance advisor the following questions if you currently have or are shopping for any type of cash value policy:

- What is my current cash value and how does it compare with the cash value shown on the illustration I signed when I applied for the policy?

- What is the difference between my cash value and my cash surrender value?

- Is my cash value held in a general account owned by the insurance company or in a separate sub-account held outside of the insurance company assets? There is a difference between an insurance company's general account and a separate sub-account. An insurance company's general account is accessible by the company's creditors; insurance company sub-accounts are not part of the insurance company's general account and therefore are not accessible by the insurance company's creditors.

- Are the illustrated projections based on a *guaranteed* rate of return, established by the insurance company that cannot be changed; a *current* rate of return, which can be changed by the insurance company; or a *projected* rate of return, which is based on the performance of the investments inside a variable policy?

- How will these different projections impact my policy now and in the future? If I can't pay the premium, how could that affect the life span of the insurance policy?

- Can my policy lapse, even if I pay the originally projected premiums?

- How does my policy loan work and what is the true cost of the loan? All cash value policies have the ability to loan money, and all have a cost associated with the loan.

- When I die or if I surrender my policy, what is the impact on my outstanding policy loans?

- How long do I want to pay a life insurance premium? How will I pay that premium in retirement or if I become disabled?

- Can I purchase a disability rider to pay my life insurance premium, if I become totally disabled? How much of the actual premium cost does it pay?

USING LIFE INSURANCE FOR ESTATE PLANNING PURPOSES

Life insurance has traditionally been a stable foundation for estate planning, due to its ability to provide liquidity when it is needed. If the life insurance is in a trust, a review of the trust should take place when you have a change in marital status, you have a change in the status and number of beneficiaries, you have a change in trustees or fiduciaries, you are relocating to another state, or you experience a substantial change in net worth.

ESTATE PLANNING CONSIDERATIONS

- If the policy is in a trust, is it a revocable or an irrevocable trust?

- Who will be the owner, beneficiary, and backup beneficiaries of the policy?

- In the event of death, disability, divorce, resignation of trustee, or firing of trustee, who will be the successor trustee for each category?

- Who would raise your minor children, and who would be responsible for paying bills and managing their inheritance?

- Are you complying with gifting laws and completing the appropriate gifting forms?

- Based on current funding and earnings assumptions, how long will the policies will last?

- Are the insurance proceeds protected from creditors?

- How do you want your personal assets distributed? If you plan on disinheriting a family member, state that and what the reason is in writing, so there can be no question about why that person is not included in the inheritance.

- If you were to become incapacitated, who would you want to carry out your financial decisions and tasks on your behalf?

When dealing with tax, estate, and insurance issues, advisors should be consulted before making any final decisions. Before you consider exchanging one life insurance contract for another, all aspects of the exchange should be considered, including cost, guaranteed and non-guaranteed interest rates, dividends, surrender charges, rider costs, cash value, insurance charges, possible rating changes, and the different features and benefits of the two policies.

ILLUSTRATIONS AND PROPOSALS

Cash value life insurance products are generally sold by illustration; the insurance company is required to provide illustrations to show you how the policy works. They are put together by the product development team, reviewed by the compliance department, sometimes packaged with a brochure from the marketing team, and given to the sales force to sell. They can be difficult to understand and difficult to compare with other illustrations.

Term life policies do not accumulate any cash value; you are just paying over a specific period of time for a death benefit. Most people think that when the term portion of a term policy is over, the policy is finished. This is not true; the policy continues but the fixed premium period is over. The premium then changes each year after the initial fixed period ends.

Depending on your age, at the end of the fixed premium period, your premium can increase substantially from the original amount. Each year, the premium continues to increase. The only reason to keep such a policy is if you are close to death.

Many companies offer a guaranteed conversion rider on their term policies. Should you become less healthy or uninsurable, you will still have the option to convert your term policy to a cash value policy without any medical and financial underwriting or evidence of insurability. Again, all conversion riders are not necessarily created equal. Know and understand the small print before you buy any type of term life insurance. If you currently own or will be buying a term life insurance policy, understand what will happen when the guaranteed term premium ends.

Differences between companies and policies:

Some policies only offer a conversion privilege from a term policy to a cash value for the first ten years of the contract. Others offer this up to age 65, and some to age 70.

Some policies offer the privilege to convert to any type of cash value policy they offer. Each insurance company offers a specific contract enabling you to switch to whatever polices they offer at that point in time, or restricted to certain policies, or only to a specific policy, which can be more expensive than a competitor's similar policy.

Some types of conversion policies can be more expensive because your insurance provider does not want to take on additional risk. Your insurance advisor can guide you.

When is the right time to purchase life insurance?

Purchase life insurance when you have someone else to protect, when you want to lock in your insurability, and when you are healthy. Sometimes clients ask agents to compare different companies and products on a spreadsheet, but compliance does not allow spread sheeting because the information can be manipulated; clients can be misled by what's included and omitted. Also, with so many assumptions and plan designs, an accurate spreadsheet would have to include so many disclosures it would be rendered useless.

A trusted advisor can guide you through the process of comparing policy offerings by interpreting complex language and marketing speech.

BENEFITS OF A PRELIMINARY
LIFE INSURANCE INQUIRY REQUEST

When you inquire about life insurance, your medical records are gathered, a new medical exam and blood/urine profile is ordered, and a generic application form is completed and signed. This inquiry package is sent to prospective insurance companies for evaluation. This allows underwriters from the companies you are considering to determine whether or not you are medically qualified to have them underwrite. This is preferable to making a formal application because:

1. It will tell you what companies appear competitive.

2. It saves time compared to shopping one company at a time.

3. Since this is an informal process, application results do not show up as either "rated" or "declined" on your medical underwriting file.

MEDICAL INFORMATION BUREAU (MIB)

Every time you go to a doctor and use your insurance company to pay for the visit, an MIB record is kept of that visit and the diagnostic codes associated with it. Keep your own record of all your doctor visits and have them available so you can provide accurate information to the medical examiner when applying for insurance.

'SCRIP CHECK

When your insurance company pays for a prescription at a pharmacy, a record is kept of that prescription. Even if you decide not to take the medicine, the record remains and you will have to explain why you were prescribed that medication, took the medication home, and didn't take it. An insurance company will generally go back up to five years to review medical and 'scrip records if you have a medical history that requires review.

JUST THE FACTS: MEDICAL RECORDS
WITHOUT THE DRAMA

When you apply for any type of insurance policy that requires medical underwriting, your insurance company underwriter may request copies of your medical file. This file includes tests performed and doctors' notes. Complaints and unresolved health issues in your underwriting file could cause an underwriter to postpone processing your insurance request until the issue of concern or requested test is performed and satisfactory results are sent to the underwriter. Or your request may receive a less attractive underwriting approval with a higher premium. You may even be declined for coverage.

RULE OF THUMB REGARDING DOCTORS WHO ARE NOT "THERAPISTS"

Unless your doctor *is* your therapist, don't make him or her your therapist. The more open-ended issues there are in your medical file, the more you will have to explain and/or document each issue, thus potentially raising the cost of your insurance. Your doctors are obligated to record your complaints and comments. These complaints in your medical file can create questions in the medical underwriter's mind about concerns and issues that may not be warranted.

LIFE INSURANCE AND PEACE OF MIND

"How inexpensively can I get through the insuring process and make my spouse happy?" This shortsighted approach generally leads to a quick term insurance purchase for a time period that could be much less than the number of years you may live. Often, this does not provide enough coverage if you die within that timeframe. The agent gets the sale, you get the life insurance coverage and premium you want, and your spouse or beneficiary gets some security for the time being. But why die without enough coverage in place when you had the opportunity to properly address this issue?

One couple had an inexpensive, minimally acceptable amount of term life insurance. Their agent told them for many years that the husband and breadwinner of the family were underinsured. Because he was healthy, he thought that life insurance was a waste of money and that he would likely outlive any term insurance policy.

One day the agent got a call from the wife. Her close friend's husband had died suddenly from a heart attack. She was in tears. "I want more life insurance now." The agent worked with the couple to find the best compromise between coverage, term, and budget. Now the husband understood what his premature death could do to his wife. Wiser choices. Peace of mind.

NEW SERVICE AGENTS

When your original agent has left the insurance company, you will eventually get a call or a letter from another agent with that company telling you he is your new service agent. Ask that agent to order an "in force" proposal for you. This will tell you how your policy is performing. If your prior agent has been proactive, you may already know this answer. If not, ask the agent to create competitive options from both your existing company and other companies. Evaluate them carefully to make choices that meet your needs going forward.

The last question to ask the agent is, *"If I never decide to purchase anything new from you, will you continue to service my account?"* If the answer is yes, have them explain to you what that exactly means. You will know from the answer whether your new service agent will continue as your service agent.

One husband had an old life insurance policy. His original agent left the company so his file was assigned to a new service agent. Because the wife was the policy owner, she received a call from the new service agent explaining that her existing policy was not performing as well as it had been projected to perform when it was first taken out. The new agent wanted to review the policy with her.

The wife did not include her husband in meetings, and she decided to replace their current policy with a new policy, one similar to the type of policy the new agent said was not performing well. No effort was made by the replacing agent to determine if they even needed the coverage. The husband went along with the replacement. They probably didn't need the policy, but the new agent got a sale, the wife got to be in control, and the husband got to appease her desire to be in control. Be proactive with your team so that you never need to be in this situation.

LOCKING IN YOUR GOOD HEALTH NOW

What happens if you purchase less than the amount of life insurance your family really needs, and you become highly rated or uninsurable after that? Your ability to purchase additional coverage may be curtailed or become more expensive than you can afford. At that point, you could need life insurance the most and not be able to purchase any more.

Many term life insurance policies have what is called a "guaranteed insurability option." This allows you to convert your term insurance policy to a cash value permanent policy without evidence of medical insurability. This is where it can get tricky; all term policies are not created equal.

There are no free lunches in term insurance. Usually the richer the options, the more expensive the premiums are for the initial term period. Often, more expensive term products turn out to be less expensive if your intention is to keep and convert the policy in the future. If you are young, fearless, and invincible, your ego may say, *"let's buy the least expensive term policy."* But a responsible family financial advocate makes family protection decisions, not egotistic or emotional decisions. Make sure that all presentations you receive properly discuss each company's conversion options so you can thoughtfully evaluate them.

Make an informed, conscientious, and well thought-out decision to continue a policy beyond its original fixed and guaranteed term premium period. Every company has its own criteria as to how long you have to convert and what you can convert to.

DISABILITY RIDER OPTIONS

Consider how you would continue to pay your life insurance premiums if you ever became permanently disabled. How long will your policies last if you are unable to make your premium payments? Many companies offer a disability waiver rider for an additional cost when you buy the policy.

An attorney had a stroke and stopped practicing. He had a cash value policy policy, which he had purchased many years before and intended to pay into for his entire life. When he became disabled, he lived off of his disability income, but the disability policy ended when he reached age 65. After 65, continuing to make the premium payments on his life insurance policy would have been a severe burden.

Fortunately, he had purchased a disability waiver when he purchased his life insurance policy. The insurance company paid his premiums for the remainder of his life, ensuring his family the death benefit he had promised them.

Only after evaluating your assets, liabilities, debt, other sources of income, lifestyle, and ability to have another family member either create income or pay premiums plus the cost/benefit and availability of this rider can you properly evaluate your need for it. Ask your insurance advisor to discuss the disability rider option with you.

CALCULATE THE AMOUNT OF LIFE INSURANCE YOU NEED

Make a list of your monthly expenses. Determine if you passed away today, how much safe, predictable, and secure income your family would need to pay their monthly bills.

Determine what type of investment risks the surviving spouse or beneficiary would be comfortable with to produce spendable, monthly, safe, predictable income.

Divide that monthly expense amount, say $10,000/ month or $120,000/year by a rate of return you feel comfortable with, say a 3% net after-tax return.

$120,000 divided by .03 = $4,000,000 of life insurance needed. If you are young, this life insurance amount should be increased to account for inflation. If you have student loans or debt, this amount should be increased accordingly. If you want to include proceeds for college education for your children, that amount should be added. If you have no children and a professional spouse or if you have substantial assets saved up, this amount can be decreased accordingly.

CONTESTABILITY PERIOD AND FRAUD

All life insurance policies have two-year contestability periods as mandated by law. A contestability period is the time from the date of policy issue that the insurance company has to contest a claim payment if the insured dies within two years of the date of the start of the policy. The insurance company has the right to review the application for fraud during this period.

If the insurance company can prove fraud and/or that the applicant had known of additional health, financial, and/or hazardous activity at the time of application, the insurance company may decide not to pay the claim and will refund the premium payments made to the beneficiary. After two years from the date of the policy, the insurance company no longer has the right to contest payment for a death claim, even if the applicant did commit fraud while completing the life insurance application.

In one interesting case, the insured was murdered before the two years were up. The insurance company was concerned that if the murderer benefited from the death, the policy could be contested and the $10M claim wouldn't be paid. After the investigation was completed, and the beneficiary was no longer under investigation for the murder, the claim was paid.

CONTESTABILITY PERIOD AND SUICIDE

That contestability period also applies to suicide. An insured person committed suicide. The widow assumed she would not receive the insurance proceeds because of this suicide. The policies he had were older policies, and the insurance company's agent delivered a large check to the widow.

LOANS AND WITHDRAWALS

If done correctly, withdrawals and loans can be taken tax-free from the accumulated cash value. There is a difference between withdrawals and loans. Loans involve gains on the premiums invested, and withdrawals involve taking out money you put into the policy as premiums, called your "cost basis." Withdrawal of cost basis incurs no taxable event because you are taking out the money you paid.

Don't assume that the accumulated premiums are your cost basis. You should request an "in-force" illustration from the insurance company with a breakdown of the cost basis to determine the actual amount. Withdrawals incur no interest charges; loans usually do. The interest charge varies and usually is partially offset by loan crediting rates.[4]

Many existing policy owners have no recollection or understanding of the true costs of insurance loans and how they work. For example your loan interest rate can be 8% with a credit of 5%. Your net cost to borrow your own money is 3%, but this can actually be more if you don't do it exactly as the insurance company requires you to. This process can be complicated and is supposed to be disclosed to the owner of the policy before they purchase it.[5]

IF LIFE INSURANCE IS AN ASSET, WHY PAY INTO IT FOREVER?

If your goal is to pay off student loans, credit card debt, and your mortgage by a certain time, why pay life insurances premiums forever? Where will this money come from when you stop working or can't work anymore?

If you have any type of cash value policy, pull out the illustration you signed when you applied for it. Look at the premium line and it will tell you how long that particular policy and premium was designed to be paid. Then have your qualified insurance advisor do an insurance audit to determine how it is actually performing.

THE LIFE INSURANCE ASSESSMENT PROCESS

If you are not sure whether your current life insurance policy will continue until you die, a diagnostic audit process will help you analyze your policy and determine how long it may last before you pass away. If you don't protect your policy and your policy lapses, you will have made significant premium payments without *any* return on your investment. Your family would get *nothing* because your policy would be terminated. A life insurance diagnosis is a report card scoring how your policy is performing.

WHY DO I NEED A POLICY REVIEW?

When you originally purchased your life insurance policy, your choice was based on your goals, your budget and which company or companies your agent represented at that time. Since then, the following may have happened:

- Your needs or budget may have changed.

- The amount and timing of your premium payments may have changed from what was presented in the original illustration presented to you by your insurance agent.

- Projected rates of return may have not materialized.

- You may have received a smoker rating and are not smoking anymore.

- You may have taken out loans, disrupting your policy's performance.

- You may have been rated based on weight, lab results, or medications, and your health status may have improved.

- Underwriters have become more educated about specific health factors. Many companies now specialize in different health issues and will often have better underwriting classes available with better pricing.

- Newer, progressive products may be available now that were not available when you purchased your life insurance policies.

- You may have purchased a policy that was predicated on you making payments your entire life. What happens if you cannot or do not want to pay those premiums forever. Do you lose your coverage?

- Assessment of the current financial stability of the life insurance carrier.

- Review of titling and fiduciary compliance if the policy is in a trust.

WHY IS AN ANNUAL REVIEW CRITICAL?

Life insurance policies are assets that require review and management, but people are inclined to stay with what they have, even though they can often times improve their situation. Complacency offers strong incentives to leave things alone, and your current agent(s) may not want to open up this conversation if they didn't design the policy properly for you when they sold it to you.

- Insurance policies tend to go into a drawer or safe deposit box and stay there for many years without anyone reviewing them.

- Consumers are not aware of product and underwriting changes that take place in the industry.

- It is difficult to see and understand the difference between projected and actual returns and their impact on the length of time the policy will stay in force.

- A difference of even 1% less return over a long period of time can devastate the cash value accumulation and length of time a policy will last.

- The IRS has made it possible to transfer gains accrued inside one life insurance policy to another life insurance policy without creating a taxable event. (This is called a 1035 exchange.)

Life insurance is an asset that needs to be monitored. As with your health, what you don't know *can* hurt you. Neither life insurance carriers nor agents are obligated to monitor your policy performance relative to your original expectations or projections presented to you when you purchased your policy. Your insurance company's only obligation is to send you a scheduled premium billing and an annual policy value statement. It is not their responsibility to confirm that you received your statement or bill. It is solely your responsibility to monitor how your policy is performing. Unfortunately, policies commonly lapse unintentionally due to bounced checks, uncollected drafts due to changing bank accounts, and not notifying the insurance company with the new drafting information, and misplaced premium bills that go unpaid.

HOW DOES THE INSURANCE COMPANY PRICE COVERAGE?

Every insurance company knows based on your age, sex, and health profile, what the odds are that you will live to their mortality table projection. Term insurance is inexpensive because most of the people who purchase it don't have it in place when they die. Learn how to purchase life insurance to exceed your mortality calculation. Research insurance company ratings; death benefits are predicated on the claims-paying ability of each carrier.*

LOANS, WITHDRAWALS AND POLICY CHANGES

Loans, withdrawals, and policy changes may impact your policy's performance. Abusing these available options can get you into trouble and may cause your policy to lapse. All cash value policies have at least two columns in their illustration showing the *guaranteed crediting rate* and *current crediting rate* and *current and guaranteed expenses*. The guaranteed column describes the worst-case scenario, and the non-guaranteed column shows the current crediting rate. Some insurance agents show different company proposals with different current crediting rates, but without an "apples to apples" comparison; the higher crediting rate may not be the best policy. Higher policy charges inside the contract can more than offset the higher crediting rate, creating a more expensive policy.

Cash value policy illustrations offer a *cash* value column and a *cash surrender* value column. The cash

---

* The rating agencies are A.M. Best, Moody's, Standard and Poor, and Fitch.

value reflects the buildup of cash inside the policy, and the cash surrender value reflects the amount of cash you would walk away with if you decided to terminate the policy.

It traditionally requires about 15 years until the cash surrender value equals the cash value. With institutional grade life insurance, the cash surrender value may be equal to or greater than the cash value in the first year of the contract. These contracts are available with universal life and variable life insurance policies. Certain restrictions and minimum funding requirements apply.

It is important to understand how policy guarantees work. With some life insurance contracts, not paying the designated premium on time can reduce, disrupt, or destroy guarantees. The key to understanding policy loans is to calculate the real cost of the loan. Have your insurance agent explain to you how the loan works, what the costs are, and what impact loans can have on your policy if you never pay back the loan.

LIFE INSURANCE AND LONG-TERM CARE (LTC) PROTECTION CAN BE A COST-EFFICIENT COMBINATION

Some life insurance policies offer long-term care riders at additional cost. Think of this rider as a long-term illness rider where you can use the death benefit to pay for your care just as you would use a separate long-term care insurance policy when you qualified for care. These types of policies are called "linked-benefit" policies because two benefits (life and long-term care) are linked together. They are valuable to people who have objections to purchasing traditional long-term care policies.

Some objections to purchasing a long-term care policy are:

- **Use it or lose it objection:** "What happens if I die and never use the policy?" In a linked benefit policy, you and/or your family will receive the entire benefit as LTC or life insurance.

- **Pricing objection:** "It's too expensive." A linked benefit policy usually costs a little less than half of what buying separate life insurance and long-term care policies as standalone policies costs.

- **Non-guarantee of premium objection:** All in-dependent LTC contracts allow the insurance company to petition the State Insurance Commissioner in that state for a premium increase for a specific group of policyholders. In some life contracts, the LTC premium is guaranteed by the insurance company.

A hybrid policy is a life insurance contract with a long-term care rider. These riders can differ and you should evaluate them with your insurance agent.

Combined Life and Long-term Care policies can be used in business situations to fund buy/sell agreements, key person policies, and other corporate arrangements. Linked benefit policies offer a way to leverage premium dollars to achieve multiple goals.

PROS AND CONS OF OWNING ONE POLICY THAT PROVIDES BOTH DEATH AND LONG-TERM CARE BENEFITS

Pros

- Can be cost effective., often less than half the price of separate life and LTC policies.

- Eliminates the "use it or lose it" objection of LTC insurance.

- Because it is a life insurance policy, the premium may not be subject to increases as a LTC policy would be.

- Both the LTC benefit and life insurance proceeds are tax-free, if titled properly.

- Builds up cash value subject to the particular policy and amount of premium you choose.

- Premiums can be structured to have the policy continue to age 125, if you choose to.

- Cash value is asset-protected from creditors in many states.

Cons

- The total coverage is the amount of the death benefit. If you use the entire death benefit amount for care, there will be no life insurance benefit remaining for the beneficiaries.

- Since it is a life insurance policy, there are no riders available for the LTC component including an inflation rider. Your death benefit and long-term care benefit are fixed. No inflation rider options are available on life insurance policies.

CHAPTER 6
DISABILITY INSURANCE
The foundation for all planning

This section discusses disability insurance, including definitions of disability, how much coverage you need, how much you can qualify for, the riders available for purchase, and how the policies work. Your advisor's role is to determine what your specific needs are and to determine which are the best contract and riders for you. The benefit of having the right advisor is that if you need to use your policy, your contract will provide exactly what you thought it would.

Many lawyers consider disability income protection to be the foundation of good planning. Disability insurance planning is critical when your income depends on your ability to wake up every day and earn a living. If you lose your earning ability, it could derail you from accumulating wealth to pay bills, pay off debt, fund children's college education expenses, and prepare for retirement.

Each insurance company offers a different definition of "disability" and a different policy cost structure. Insurance companies often have subtle differences in benefits and definitions. The most important component of a disability plan is the structure of the policy. This chapter explains how to work with your advisor to determine which coverage is best for you.

DISABILITY INSURANCE AS AN ASSET: NO WORK; NO INCOME

What is disability insurance?

Disability insurance is both an asset and income protection, similar to life insurance. You can usually protect up to 60% of your gross earned income. This earned income can include wages; salary, bonuses, profit sharing, and pension plan contributions. Be sure to document all sources of income that could assist you in qualifying when you apply for coverage. If you are unable to perform the duties of your job, (also called the "material and substantial duties of your primary occupation") due to an accident or illness, you will be able to apply for this benefit.

How do you qualify?

You will have to go through medical underwriting unless the policy is part of a guarantee issue corporate group plan. In a guarantee issue plan, all employees are eligible to participate, regardless of their health history, up to the dollar limits established by the insurance company.

The medical underwriting will include a paramedical exam and blood and urine profile. The urine profile is a tobacco and drug screening. The financial underwriting will include two years of W-2s, income tax earnings if you are employed, and your entire personal and corporate tax returns if you are self-employed and derive income from several sources.

Definitions of disability

Every company has its own marketing name and definition of what total disability is. Seek coverage based on your legal specialty, called "own occupation," so if you cannot work in that specialty, you'll have the right to collect your entire monthly benefit along with the choice to work doing anything else you want without losing any of your disability income.

For example, an attorney might be forced to quit practicing trial work if his health rendered it impossible to be in a trial, but that same attorney might become a researcher or document attorney who can work without the intensity and stress of trial. Or he may choose to become a professional photographer outside the legal profession. By tying his policy to his ability to work as a specific type of attorney, he will continue to receive benefits, even if he finds alternative employment.

Waiting period, called an elimination period

The waiting period is the time you have to wait from the time your medical impairment is diagnosed to the time you will start receiving your monthly disability payments. You can buy a policy with a specific waiting period, usually 30, 60, 90, 180, or 365 days. 90 days is generally the most cost-effective.

Benefit period or how long the company will pay you

You can purchase coverage to pay until you reach age 65, 67, or 70. Lifetime coverage may be available from some carriers. Many lifetime contracts provide decreasing coverage, as you get older. Evaluate the different benefit options with your insurance professional.

Partial disability rider

Partial disability is also called "residual disability." When you lose 20% of your income due to injury or sickness, you could be considered partially disabled. Conversely, if you lose 80% of your income, you could be considered permanently disabled.

Caution: If you do not have this rider, you are either fully disabled or you are not. This means if you lose up to 80% of your income, you might not be covered for any illness or injury you incur. You must lose 80% *or more* of your income to qualify for total disability without a partial disability rider. You will be self-insuring your partial loss of income.

Cost of Living Adjustment (COLA)

If you don't have this rider, you will have a specific monthly benefit coming to you for the life of your contract. If you purchase this rider when you purchase your policy, your coverage can increase per the terms of this rider, when your claim starts.

Several inflation compensation options may be available. These options usually range from 2% to

7% annual increases and a choice of simple inflation or compound inflation. Compound inflation riders are more expensive than simple inflation riders. For example:

5% simple could be $10,000/month x 5% = $10,500/month. Next year benefit is $11,000

5% compound could be $10,000/month x 5% = $10,500. Next year benefit is $11,250.

With 5% simple interest, your disability payment will increase in this example $500 per year.

With 5% compound interest, your disability payment will increase based on prior years benefit.

Discuss Cost of Living Riders costs and benefits with your insurance advisor.

Guaranteed Insurability

You can purchase more coverage in the future if your income increases without evidence of insurability by locking in your current health underwriting status. This benefit is called "guaranteed insurability," and this increase in coverage is based on your increased income, regardless of health.

Catastrophic coverage

If you lose two or more limbs or your sight or hearing, you will receive an additional monthly benefit if you have this rider in place.

Automatic benefit coverage

Even if your income never increases, you can purchase a rider that will increase your coverage by a pre-determined rate for a certain number of years. With some policies, this rider is included in your base policy.

Limitation of benefits for mental/nervous and substance abuse disorders

This "*mental and nervous*" clause specifies that if you become disabled for stress related reasons; your policy will only pay your monthly benefit for two years. In essence this becomes a two-year benefit plan if your claim is based on a stress-related condition.

Understand what you are giving away in coverage if you accept this limitation. You lose the opportunity to receive disability income beyond two years if you become disabled due to a mental or emotional issue that prevents you from doing your job.

Though it can be uncomfortable to insist on benefits that suggest you doubt your ability to remain mentally functional or abstain from substance abuse, stress-related disability can strike anyone subject to overwhelming stressful conditions beyond their control. Discuss this rider with your insurance agent and make an objective decision about whether or not you want these limitations in your policy.

Waiver of premium provision

If you file a disability claim, your premium payment will stop. If you go off-claim, your premium payment will start again and your coverage will continue.

Male/Female/Unisex rates

Female's rates for disability are more expensive than males'. Most insurance companies offer unisex rates or a "*blended rate*" that is less expensive for females if three or more employees of a group sign up for coverage. These can be male or female employees, and the male can get a slightly lower rate as part of a group discount. Speak to your insurance agent about discounts that may be in place for you either at work or through associations you belong to.

Disability Income Insurance Misconceptions

"*I am young and in good health now.*"

"I could do my job from my hospital bed or from home."

"I should only purchase enough protection to cover my current expenses."

"I am covered through my group disability income insurance policy offered through my company, and don't need to consider any more."

"My spouse works or could go back to work if I couldn't."

"I have savings to cover me if I couldn't work."

Ask yourself: "If this disability actually happened to me, would I be OK or would I wish I had the extra income from a disability policy?"

Benefit offset provisions between group and individual disability coverage

This factor is important to review if you have or are considering obtaining both group and individual disability coverage. Some group policies have an offset provision that says if you also collect from an individual policy or social security, the insurance company will subtract that amount from your group coverage. Additionally, many individual policies have caps on coverage so, for example, if their total cap is $20,000 per month and you have group coverage of $10,000 per month, they will only issue you $10,000 per month of individual coverage, even though you could have qualified for $15,000 per month of individual coverage based on your earned income.

Discuss these provisions with your advisor. There's no point in paying for any more coverage than you're eligible to receive.

Pre-existing health condition

Pre-existing conditions can be related to spine, back, or musculoskeletal problems that can make you more susceptible to filing a claim. Such a condition could be excluded, require a surcharge, or both. Usually insurance companies will review your medical file after two years if you ask them. If your medical situation has improved, they will take that into consideration to see if an exclusion or extra premium is still required. You can always appeal again down the road if your situation improves. If your health does improve and you don't review and manage your policy regularly, you could continue to pay more for limited coverage.

COST OF COVERAGE

To get a good basic policy, budget 2% of your gross income for the policy. If you are older than 50 or are looking for more robust benefits, budget 3-4% of your gross income.

Guaranteed renewable vs. a non-cancelable policy

In a guaranteed renewal contract, the premiums are less expensive in the beginning, but they can increase, compared to a non-cancellable policy where premiums are guaranteed never to increase. Ask your insurance agent to help you weigh the pros and cons of each type of policy.

Level premium vs. annual increasing premium

With a **guaranteed level premium,** your premium is fixed and guaranteed for the life of the contract.

With a **non-guaranteed level premium,** your premium is fixed but *can* be increased subject to your insurance company being approved by the State Insurance Commissioner to raise premiums.

With an **annual increasing premium,** your premium starts out lower and gradually increases. This policy is for people whose cash flow is tight, but who will be able to afford a greater premium down the road.

Retirement Income Benefit

This benefit will fund your pension plan up to your current contributions until you're age 65 and then that money is yours to use for retirement. This benefit helps you financially prepare for retirement if you can't work.

Recurrent disability benefit coverage

Every policy has an elimination or waiting period. If you become disabled but then recover and return to work and then become disabled again, do you start your waiting period again when you start your disability coverage again? Each policy will define the parameters of a recurrent disability. Make sure your insurance agent explores such possibilities and helps you select the coverage you need.

Taxation of benefits

If you pay for coverage with after-tax dollars (money you have already paid income tax on), benefits are tax-free. If your employer or your corporation pays the premium and takes a tax deduction, then the benefit will be taxable to you.

Helpful hint: If your company pays the premium, ask them to issue you a 1099 income tax form at the end of the year for the premium so you will be responsible for paying the income tax on that premium. This way, if you become disabled, the benefit will be tax-free to you, instead of taxable.

SPECIAL DISABILITY PROGRAMS
FOR NEW LAWYERS

Discounts vary by state and are not available in all states. These are individual, not group, policies that you own and you can take them to any state in which you end up working. Regardless of income, you can receive up to $6,500 a month in coverage to start out. Lawyers can obtain policies that can neither be cancelled nor altered once they are issued. Your premiums can be guaranteed and fixed until the contract ends or you cancel it. Exact terms of contracts will vary by state.

Ask your insurance advisor about special programs and discounts for legal professionals. Your occupation is unique and special coverage programs should be evaluated carefully.

Guarantee issue group contracts

These types of contracts can be valuable if you have severe health issues or are uninsurable.

- The Good: No medical underwriting.

- The Bad: Gender-distinct rates; unisex rates are usually not available with this program.

- The Ugly: Contracts usually have a 24-month limitation for mental and nervous disability.

Business disability coverage for Buy-Sell Agreements and office overhead.

These provisions cover the buyout of a disabled partner's stock. You can choose one of three elimination or waiting periods of 12, 18, and 24 months. You can have a payout option of a lump sum payout, or a down payment with equal monthly installments made over five years, or equal monthly payments made over a five-year period with no down payment. This type of coverage is usually available up to age 60.

Business Overhead Coverage covers office expenses, including salaries of all employees not including the owner lawyer. Employees may be covered. This coverage is usually available for 12 months. Several companies offer coverage up to $50,000 per month for approved office-related expenses. Specialized coverage is available for overhead needs beyond $50,000 per month.

CHAPTER 7
LONG-TERM CARE (LTC)
INSURANCE

"… I hope I die before I get old …"
—Pete Townshend, Fabulous Music, Ltd.

Will you get old before you die? Should you insure this risk? What options do you have? What types of policies are available and what riders will you need? An advisor's role is to help you determine if you can or want to self-insure this risk. The right advisor will present viable options and design plans so you can evaluate the costs/benefits of managing this risk.

According to the U.S. Department of Health and Human Services,[†] nearly 70% of men and women turning 65 will need some form of long-term care at some point in their lives.

Elder care planning preserves dignity by planning ahead for aging loved ones. What can be more digni-

† http://longtermcare.gov

fied than staying in your home as long as you can? We all want to age with dignity, freedom of choice, and independence.

Think about long-term care insurance *before:*

- An adult child becomes the parent to a parent or you no longer know if a parent is taking or being given the correct medicine(s).

- Mom or Dad can no longer live independently and with dignity, or when forgetfulness becomes chronic or terminal illness is involved.

- The checkbook is a mess or it's time to give up the car key.

- You live in another state and can only care from afar, or the caregivers are experiencing wear and tear.

Cognitive Impairment is a deficiency in a person's short or long-term memory; orientation as to person, place and time; deductive or abstract reasoning; or judgment as it relates to their safety and awareness. Dementia is a deterioration of intellectual capacity due to a disorder of the brain.

Alzheimer's is a form of dementia that causes problems with memory, thinking, behavior and motor skills. Alzheimer's disease is an irreversible, progressive brain disease that slowly destroys memory and thinking skills, and eventually the ability to carry out the simplest tasks and responsibilities. Short-term memory loss is the most prevalent early symptom of the disease. Prior to these conditions becoming serious, it is important to start creating advanced planning. Do this with your loved ones by clarifying how they want to be taken care of when they can no longer take care of themselves. Have a family meeting to locate and organize all important and legal documents.

LTC CONSIDERATIONS

A Living Will records a person's wishes for medical treatment near the end of his life.

A Living Trust provides instructions about the person's estate and appoints a trustee to hold title to property and assets for the person who inherits them.

A Durable Power of Attorney for Health Care designates an agent to make healthcare decisions when the person no longer can.

A Durable Power of Attorney for Financial Matters names someone to make financial decisions when the person no longer can.

A Do Not Resuscitate Order (DNR) instructs healthcare professionals not to perform cardiopulmonary resuscitation if a person's heart or breathing stops. A DNR order is signed by a doctor and put in the person's chart.

Elder Law Attorneys specialize in this type of law. They can guide you through the legal minefield and attention to details.

A long-term care event is when someone has a prolonged physical illness, a disability, or a cognitive impairment. Long-term care insurance is applied when a person is unable to perform two out of six specific Activities of Daily Living (ADL's). These are bathing, eating, dressing, toileting, continence, and transferring (into or out of bed). Cognitive impairment (such as dementia or Alzheimer's) is a standalone reason to qualify for long-term care.

How have low interest rates and longer lifespans affected insurance companies?

Life insurance companies invest your premiums to generate income. In a low interest rate environment, their rates of return are lower and can have a negative impact on their profitability. As a result, insurance companies can be forced to discontinue certain policies and offer new policies that are usually more expensive and/or offer fewer benefits.

TYPES OF LONG-TERM CARE INSURANCE

Reimbursement model

Reimbursement offers a fixed amount of coverage. If you incur an expense that's less than the allowable coverage, the insurance company will pay only that amount of benefit.

Indemnity model

Indemnity offers a fixed amount of coverage. The benefit is not based on a specific service received or expense incurred.

Cash or disability model

This type of policy offers the most flexibility in receiving payments. You are only required to meet benefit eligibility criteria. Once you do, you'll receive your full daily benefit, even if you are not receiving any long-term care services. In the USA, this supplements your social security benefit.

WHEN DOES COVERAGE BEGIN?

Different companies offer a choice of 0, 20, 30, 60, 90 or 100-day elimination or waiting period before coverage starts. You are responsible for self-insuring the costs of coverage until your benefit starts. Your insurance advisor will review the cost benefit of each of these options, your financial capacity, and willingness to self-insure the elimination period when you will not yet be receiving money from the insurance company.

RIDERS

Inflation rider starts building up immediately. You do not have to wait until the policy starts, like disability insurance to start benefiting from the increased coverage.

Survivorship rider is available for married couples. This allows the surviving spouse to use any benefits you have left after you passed away.

Additional Cash rider can be used for any expenses or you can save the money.

Waiver of Premium rider means that your premium payments will stop when your payments start.

Restoration of Benefits rider means that if you go on a claim and recover, usually after 6 months of being recovered, the insurance company will restore the money they paid out to your account.

Combination life insurance and Long-term Care (LTC) benefit life insurance policies and **annuity policies** are available. Under these policies, a portion of the death benefit is accelerated (received early) tax-free should someone need care at home or in a facility. The LTC withdrawal benefit is determined at the time a policy is issued and is specified in the contract.

FACTS ABOUT LONG-TERM CARE

Men's and women's policies are priced differently. Women live longer than men on average. For life insurance purposes, women are less expensive than men. For LTC purposes, women are more expensive than men.

LTC is a *"use it or lose it"* policy. If you die before you use it, the benefit is never received.

Premiums are fixed, but not guaranteed. All insurance companies have the right to ask the State

Insurance Commissioner in your state to increase the price of a block of business if the financial soundness of the insurance company is in jeopardy.

For tax qualified long-term care plans, benefits you receive are not considered taxable income. Additionally, you may deduct long term care premiums as medical expenses subject to IRS guidelines. Please consult your accountant and the Federal Long Term Care Insurance Program for details.

The 2016 IRS Tax limits for Long-term Care Insurance: [‡]

- Age 40 or less $390
- Age 41 to age 50 ....$730
- Age 51 to age 60................................. $1,460
- Age 61 to age 70................................. $3,900
- Age 71 and older $4,870

HOME HEALTH AGENCIES
AND NURSE REGISTRIES

Inevitably, people who cannot take care of themselves require professional assistance. Long-term Care Insurance can pay for this professional help. There are two categories of care:

A **Home Health Agency** is a company that offers skilled nursing services and at least one other

‡. www.aaltci.org/guides

therapeutic service in the home of the client. The nurses and staff are usually employees of the agency and therefore the agency provides liability and workman's compensation insurance as well as taking care of employer/employee related taxes.

A Nurse Registry is a company that supplies registered nurses, licensed practical nurses, certified nursing assistants, home health aides, companions, or homemakers who are paid by the registry as independent contractors. The registry assumes no financial responsibility for the person you hire.

If you hire a caregiver, you are considered an employer. As an employer, you should withhold Social Security, Medicare, and Federal and State taxes, if applicable, from the caregiver's pay. You also need to contribute employment taxes, matching Social Security, Medicare, and unemployment taxes. Additionally, the homeowner may be liable for issues in the home resulting from slip and fall or injury to the caregiver employee. Seek legal and accounting advice before proceeding if you have any questions about hiring a caregiver.

VA AIDE AND ATTENDANCE PENSION§

The Veteran's Administration offers a special qualification program for Veterans and/or spouses of de-

§. www.benefits.va.gov/pension

ceased veterans. A qualified applicant can get up to $24,000 annually for private duty home care and/ or assisted living rent for the rest of his life.

PROTECTION AGAINST
UNINTENDED COVERAGE LAPSES

Always have a responsible backup contact on file with the insurance company. If you move, make sure the insurance company changes your address in their system. You are responsible for making premium payments, not the insurance company.

If payments are made through auto-pay, check with the bank every couple of months to make sure premiums are still being made. If you handle the checkbook, review each monthly statement to confirm that the payment has been made. Insurers are not required to prove they have contacted a third party if premium payments are not made.

The (NAIC) National Association of Insurance Commissioners publishes a *Shopper's Guide to Long-term Care Insurance.* Get a copy from your agent and become familiar with it before you purchase any coverage or visit www.aaltci.org.

SECTION THREE SUMMARY
LIFETIME PLANNING

What do your health and your wealth have in common?

- They are both lifetime endeavors that work best with a plan and discipline.
- They both work best when a coach, trainer, or team leader is involved.
- They both can be negatively impacted by special needs and circumstances.
- They both can take a long time to create and a short time to dismantle.

Rule#1: Accumulation, distribution, and decumulation planning require different thinking and different strategies.

Rule#2: It is impossible to control or prevent unknown risks and economic breakdowns during your lifetime.

Therefore, because financial planning is not a finite planning process, contingency planning should be reviewed annually and adjusted accordingly.

Rule#3: Lifetime planning is not about how much money you can make, but how safely you can keep it.

Rule#4: The older you are, the less time you have to recover from losses. Lifetime planning should focus on protecting your downside.

Rule#5: Retirement plans can be complex. Use retirement plan professionals and pension professionals.

Rule#6: When family assets are composed of yours, mine, and ours, planning can become extremely emotional and challenging. Non-money issues and money issues can arise.

CHAPTER 8
LIFETIME INCOME PLANNING

An income stream you cannot outlive

How do you create an income stream that you cannot outlive?

Retirement involves having the ability to live a comfortable and meaningful life without the requirement of earning income.

Many lawyers are prepared to replace only a portion of their income in retirement, compared with the 70% of earned income that is recommended. Unless an attorney has clients, they often don't start earning significant paychecks until well into their careers. At that point, they may still be carrying tuition debt, starting families, and buying homes, which can discourage savings. Yet attorneys increased income leads them to expect high living standards in retirement.

Retirement planning begins with retirement *forecasting,* which is loaded with assumptions. You can only make decisions about the future from the present. You have to anticipate when you will retire, how long you will live, and what it will cost in tomorrow's dollars, adjusted for inflation. Until it commences, the notion of retirement can be an abstract future concept.

Lifetime income planning considers your assets, your liabilities, and your potential, possible, and predictable income during retirement. An advisor's role is to provide a realistic breakdown of your lifestyle needs and to define what income strategies fit best. An advisor experienced in *distribution* planning can be a different advisor from one who is experienced in *accumulation* planning. Wealth building, wealth management, and wealth preservation require different strategies.

Retirement is not just about net worth or assets; it is about receiving lifetime income. You spend your working career diligently accumulating assets so you can live off of them. Because retirement is a distribution plan, it's about taking money *out,* not about putting money *in.* Without the help of a wealth management team, lifetime income planning can be more difficult than accumulating assets.

The retirement process officially starts when you switch from saving to spending your savings in order to support yourself for the remainder of your life. This is *distribution* or *decumulation* or *spending down* your assets planning. It requires a different set of skills and planning processes with their own set of risks and unknowns. By retirement, you should have a lifestyle-spending plan in place. The process can be complicated; retirement withdrawal strategies can be complex with a lot of unknowns and assumptions.

When you are retired, every day is Saturday. This is the end game; the money you worked so hard to earn and accumulate is only the scorecard. Spend your life wisely preparing for retirement in the style you desire and deserve. Enjoy retirement with a sense of control and clarity Within the next 10 years, 70 million baby boomers will begin to see if they planned it right.

TRADE LIFESTYLE NOW
FOR LIFESTYLE IN THE FUTURE

Attorneys should plan to put away 20% of their income to prepare to retire in the lifestyle to which they are accustomed. If you are ambitious and want to retire at age 60, consider putting 25% of your income away every year. When you think about retirement, look at the issues you will have to address: Where will you live and what will the cost of living be?

Consider city and state income taxes, if applicable, and the average cost of a home. The climate, cultural amenities, access to high quality healthcare, and the costs associated with that healthcare, transportation, crime rates, etc. will impact your retirement years.

DURABLE INCOME

The more investment reward we want, the more investment risk we have to take on. A wise retirement strategy achieves desired financial goals with the least amount of risk. Durable income is a strategy for maximizing the performance of a traditional retirement portfolio to maintain the income necessary to fund the lifestyle you want throughout retirement. The goal is to incorporate various investment classes to optimize the risk-return performance of having stocks, bonds and fixed-income investments.

The goal of any retirement strategy is to deliver predictable and acceptable financial results on a continuous basis. A comprehensive financial strategy should address principal protection, inflation contingencies, tax efficiency, long-term growth, and lifetime income. A comprehensive strategy looks at your investments in light of market cycles and market corrections. Market volatility often brings havoc to a retirement distribution strategy.

RISK TOLERANCE

Every decision in life has risk attached to it. We will always have competing risks. What risks are you willing to accept? Is there such a thing as unnecessary investment risk? Should you invest to achieve maximum gain or only take on the amount of risk you need to achieve an intended result? Ask your retirement advisor about the potential impact of risk-adjusted returns, average returns, and sequence of returns on your retirement strategy.

Risk *management* is different than risk *tolerance.* Unless your emotions, your spouse's emotions, your ego, your financial picture, and your lifestyle are authentic and connected, you run the risk of either investing too aggressively or too conservatively for your personal comfort level. Risk profile forms assist you and your advisor in objectively determining your risk profile. These forms are only a guide; you must make the final decision on your comfort regarding risk.

WITHDRAWAL RISK

During retirement, you will no longer be working but your investments will continue to go up, and down. 2000 to 2010 became known as the "*lost decade*"; it took approximately 10 years for certain stock market indexes to return to where they were in 2000. What challenges did investors who retired in 1999 face? What challenges will *you* face?

EMOTIONS AND IGNORANCE CREATE ERRORS

Professional monitoring is important.

- Understand the concept of *timing* the market versus *time in* the market and compound interest versus simple interest.

- Don't let the stock market determine your risk tolerance by following the herd or by letting greed or fear be your basis for investing.

- Understand that return *of* your money is different than return *on* your money.

- Understand the appropriate timelines for investing: short term (1-3 years), intermediate term (4-7 years), and long-term (8+ years).

RISK BASED ASSET ALLOCATION

Asset allocation means your investments are spread across different asset classes such as stocks, bonds, and cash equivalents to manage risk and help decrease return volatility. An "asset class" is a group of securities that have similar risk/return characteristics and that behave similarly when your investments go up and down. Create a mix of asset classes that work well together to help you meet your long-term objectives.

RISK BASED ASSET LOCATION

Asset location means your investments are located in the right asset categories for income tax considerations. For example, some investments are designed for long-term goals such as retirement. Some investments are designed for short-term investments like buying a home. Investments for short-term use should be safer. Investments for long-term goals should be more aggressive. Investments like stocks where you can generate more favorable tax treatment if held for more than a year should be utilized, for long-term planning.

CORRELATION OF ASSETS

Correlation of assets shows how two investments move in relation to one other. Is your correlation of asset classes low or high? If the stock market suddenly decreased 30%, would your investment portfolio go down 30%? In 2008, many asset classes that were supposed to be low correlation turned out to be high correlation. Many people took on higher risk than they thought and therefore incurred higher losses.

PORTFOLIO MONITORING
VERSUS PORTFOLIO MANAGEMENT

Portfolio *monitoring* looks backward, examining a portfolio in terms of investment performance and results. Portfolio *management* looks forward. By doing both, decisions can be made about various securities and asset classes that are designed to match your portfolio with your personal objectives and investment risk tolerance.

7 QUESTIONS TO DISCUSS WITH
YOUR ADVISOR ABOUT INVESTMENTS

Understanding the answers to these questions is critical to being an educated investor and participating in the decision-making process regarding your money.

1. How do I know how much investment risk I can handle?

2. What are the differences between average annual returns vs. sequence of returns?

3. What are the differences between asset allocation and asset location?

4. What is the difference between active and passive management?

5. What are the differences between secular bull & bear markets?

6. What are the differences between fee-based and commission-based products?

7. What is "style drift" and how do I protect myself from it?

IS YOUR ADVISOR A DISTRIBUTION PLANNING PROFESSIONAL?

Many advisors focus on accumulation planning, yet retirement is about *distribution* planning. How do you know who will be the best retirement planner for you?

5 QUESTIONS YOUR RETIREMENT ADVISOR SHOULD ASK YOU ABOUT RETIREMENT

1) **What does retirement mean to you?**

At what age do you want to retire? Will you wind down or just stop practicing or working? Can you monetize your practice to create cash flow after you retire? What would that look like? What could derail it?

2) If you were incapacitated, who would handle your affairs?

What monthly spendable income will be needed to support your dream lifestyle?

3) Net worth, assets and liabilities: What do these mean to your retirement strategy?

Earned Income: Will you be working part-time?

Investment Income: Who will manage your assets in retirement?

Guaranteed Income: Will your income be guaranteed or subject to market performance?

4) What assumptions have you made to answer these questions?

What rate of inflation will you use to determine purchasing power when you retire and through your retirement? What will happen if your assumptions are incorrect? What are Plans B and C if things don't work out as intended? What will happen if you retire in a down economy and/or down stock market?

6) How many years of retirement do you want to generate income for?

Have you factored the cost of future healthcare into your budget and planning?

Do you know what the cost of assisted living is today and how many people living past age 65 require some type of LTC services?

If you already went through this exercise, which advisor validated this information for you, how long ago, and when will you review these questions again?

RETIREMENT PLANS

Retirement Plans involve sophisticated areas of the law. Work with retirement plan professionals who are knowledgeable and current on all retirement strategies and tax laws.

Questions you should ask your pension advisor about retirement plans:

What types of retirement plans are there and how do they work? What are the differences between the plans and which one is best for me?

TYPES OF RETIREMENT PLANS

401(k) Defined Contribution Plan: an employer-sponsored plan established for the benefit of its employees. The employees may contribute their own money, subject to IRS guidelines. The employer may choose to contribute on a year-to-year basis. In this type of plan, the value or benefit at retirement is undefined and unknown. Your actual plan value will be based on the contributions to and performance of your investments.

The company you work for sets up this plan. As an employee, you can put your own money in up to a maximum of 15% of your income, up to a current total of $18,000 per year (2016). The money you put in is pre-tax contributions, which means you get a tax deduction on your contribution and it grows tax deferred. As long as that money stays in the plan, you do not pay any income tax on the principal investment and the gains. The money will be fully taxable at whatever your tax bracket is in the year you take the money. If you are over the age of 50, you can add another $6,000 in each year (2016), called a catch-up provision. These two amounts can increase every year subject to IRS requirements.

If you work for the government or for a not-for-profit company, this plan is called a 403B and it may operate in a similar way.

If you are a sole employee of your own company, you can set up a Uni (K) or Solo 401(K). This plan operates similarly to the 401K and 403B plan.

These plans are subject to strict IRS guidelines. Violating these guidelines can negate a plan and cause adverse tax consequences.

IRA: a personal retirement plan, used when you are self-employed or your employer does not have a retirement plan in place. This plan is subject to IRS guidelines and restrictions.

ROTH IRA: a personal retirement plan that does not offer a tax deduction in the year you invest the money. The money grows and can be taken out income tax-free subject to IRS guidelines and restrictions.

Spousal IRA: operates like a traditional IRA. A nonworking spouse can put away up to $5,500 a year on a tax-deductible basis. If you are 50 or older, she/he can put away up to a total of $6,500 per year (2016). This is a separate IRA for the spouse and it grows tax deferred until withdrawn.

SEP: a Simplified Employee Pension plan provided by an employer for the benefit of its employees.

Roth 401(k): an employer sponsored plan established for the benefit of employees. The employee

can make after-tax contributions, which means s/
he will not get a tax deduction for the contributions. The Roth 401K offers tax-deferred growth.
Tax-free withdrawals are permitted if IRS guidelines are met.

Defined Benefit Plan: an employer sponsored plan
where the benefit at retirement is known before retirement. In the private sector, defined benefit plans
are normally funded exclusively by the employer.
In the public sector, defined benefit plans often
require employee contributions to fund the plan.

Profit Sharing Plan: an employer sponsored plan
where shareholders agree to distribute profits to
employees for retirement.

*These limits can change each year. Consult your tax
advisor and employer for current limits.*

ANNUITIES

Annuities are complex financial instruments. An
annuity is designed to be an income vehicle, while
stocks, bonds, and mutual funds are designed to be
investment vehicles.

An *annuity* is a contract offered by an insurance company that provides for a series of payments to the owner (the annuitant) over a specified period of time or for life. It can help diversify a retirement portfolio by providing income stability for a fee. Annuities are designed as longevity insurance that provides an income benefit.

Annuities are very sophisticated financial instruments that may be sold by prospectus. Hypothetical illustrations may be available by request. All companies offer different variations and no two products are alike. Review and understand the features, limitations, risks, charges, expenses, investment objectives, and income distribution strategies of each with your pension or retirement advisor.[6]

Annuities are an acknowledgement by investors that in addition to brokerage and investment management companies, insurance companies can assist in managing stock market risk. Annuities can be a valuable piece of an overall retirement strategy. Some features of annuities include tax deferral; avoidance of probate; lifetime income; principal protection; wealth transfer; nursing care income; and in some states protection from creditors.

ANNUITY TERMS

Deferred Annuity: The purchase payments you make can grow tax-deferred subject to the type of annuity and guarantees purchased.

Immediate Annuity: Payments can start immediately or in one year.

Annuity certain: Can pay a specific amount for a specific period of time, with the remaining payments going to the beneficiary if the person dies before the end of the payment period.

Annuity certain for life: Can pay a specific amount for the lifetime of the person.

Cash refund annuity: Can pay a lump sum balance benefit to the beneficiary if the entire premium paid has not been received as benefits.

Fixed Annuity: The income payment is based on a fixed rate of return established by the insurance company.

Joint survivor annuity: A specified amount of income is paid until the second spouse passes away.

Indexed Annuity: Can be fixed products and therefore not sold by prospectus. There are many different types of index options, so speak to your financial advisor about what annuities are available.

Variable deferred Annuity: Payments go into a portfolio of investments you choose from a pool of options (with the help of your advisor).

Annuity companies offer riders with different benefits at additional cost, examples include:
- Guaranteed Minimum Income Benefit
- Guaranteed Minimum Death Benefit
- Ratchets: Daily, monthly, or annual high value adjustments
- Indexed growth options

Annuities are tax deferred, not tax-free. Annuities that are not owned by individuals but by an entity such as a corporation are generally not eligible for tax deferral. Seek professional guidance from your tax advisor.[8]

QUESTIONS TO ASK YOUR INSURANCE AGENT ABOUT ANNUITIES

- Is this type of investment suitable for me? Why?

- Can you give me a breakdown of the costs?

- How do annuities work?

- How do I take income out?

- What are worst case and best case scenarios?

- What other investment options do I have if I am considering an annuity?

Every company and plan design is different. Consult your advisors to determine the appropriateness of these products; what options are best for you, and costs. Review the prospectus and disclosures.

NON-QUALIFIED BENEFIT PLANS

Many corporations use life insurance as a funding vehicle for non-qualified benefit plans. Premiums are paid into corporate-owned fixed or variable universal life insurance policies with the following defining characteristics:

- In addition to paying for death benefit protection, your premiums help build cash value. You determine the asset allocation with assistance of your advisor. Generally, many options are available. Within the parameters of your policy design, you have control over the frequency of premium payments and withdrawals, which allows you to better tailor your income and retirement income needs.

- Corporate-owned life insurance (COLI) policies may differ from the load and expense structures of retail life insurance. While the cash surrender values are not guaranteed, COLI has no surrender charges. Therefore the cash value and cash surrender value may be similar based on market performance and other factors. Cash values accumulate on a tax-deferred basis and can be structured for tax-advantaged access and distribution.

- Understand that loans and withdrawals will reduce the policy's cash value and death benefit, and that withdrawals in excess of the policy's basis are taxable. The basis is the premiums you have put into the contract over its life. Under current rules, policy loans are generally income tax-free as long as the policy remains in effect until the insured's death, at which time the loan will be satisfied from the income tax-free death benefit proceeds. If the policy is surrendered, any loan balance will generally be viewed as distributable and taxable in the year of the distribution.

- There are no charges when and if you terminate the policy. You may surrender your policy any time for its cash surrender value. Any gains over and above what you put in will be taxable at ordinary income tax rates. There are no age 59-1/2 penalties on the withdrawals based on the current tax laws. Consult your tax advisor regarding the treatment of any gains and withdrawals from within your policy.

- Creditor protection exists in many states for life insurance benefits and cash values. Consult your attorney specialist for details in your state.

- Your policy has the potential to grow out of the insurer's general assets if your life insurance policy is a fixed permanent policy, or it has the potential to grow through a variety of managed investment options if your policy is a variable life policy. Neither of these options is risk-free. Your fixed options have credit risk and your variable options have market risk. Discuss the pros and cons with your insurance advisor.

A majority of Fortune 500 companies use these types of vehicles to additionally fund their key employees' retirement.

CREATING A NON-QUALIFIED
BENEFIT PROGRAM

A non-qualified benefit plan can create meaningful retirement benefits that are not restricted by government-imposed limits on benefits and participation.

With this plan design, your insurance agent tells you, "Declare the most money you are willing to put into this policy, and I will tell you how little life insurance you need to buy to qualify for it."

This policy is custom designed to create an income strategy that will accumulate and distribute supplemental retirement funds in a tax-advantaged way. For this type of policy to work properly, there are no up-front sales load or surrender charges. In addition, the cash value and cash surrender value are liquid. Minimum premium contributions are required. This sophisticated product is used in corporate America to fund deferred compensation plans, key employee funding plans, and to supplement traditional retirement funding goals.

Work with a Non-Qualified Benefits professional to see if this plan is right for you. Your benefits professional should be able to address all the steps below with you.

- Plan Design, Plan Consultation, Plan Implementation, Plan Documents, and Plan Administration.

- Policy Implementation, Policy Administration and Policy Holder Services.

- Annual reviews to review performance to benchmarks.

TAX STRATEGIES

Taxes have different categories and different implications.

Characteristics of different types of investments:

- Taxable each year.

- Tax deferred until distributed.

- Tax-free when distributed.

- Short-term capital gains tax has a lower tax rate than current tax rate.

- Long-term capital gains tax has a lower tax rate than short-term and current tax rate.

- Income tax based on your tax bracket each year.

THE 4 BIG I'S: INFLATION, INTEREST RATES, INCOME TAXES, INSTABILITY

Due to Federal Tax Rules that continue to increase and change, accomplished professional advisors are required. Over the course of your lifetime, inflation, interest rates, income taxes, and financial markets will impact your financial picture. The right advisory team will assist you in making wise decisions with your money.

11 QUESTIONS TO ASK YOUR ACCOUNTANT/TAX ADVISOR

1. Am I an employer, an employee, or both?

2. What are the tax deduction differences between

being an employer, an employee, or both?

3. What business expense tax write-offs can I benefit from if I work for myself?

4. Do I need to establish a corporation? How do I determine which type of corporation is best?

5. What benefits can I establish as a business owner and which are tax deductible?

6. How do I determine what retirement plans are right for me?

7. Which benefits are portable, (which means you can take those benefits with you if you leave your employer) and which are not?

8. Which benefits are tax-deductible and what benefits are tax-free?

9. How do I protect my business and myself from creditor judgments?

10. Should I buy my insurance as a group benefit, individual benefit, or both?

11. Explain the concept and trade-offs of tax-deductible premiums vs. tax-free benefits.

CHAPTER 9
SPECIALIZED PLANNING

Some situations require specialized advice. These circumstances include families with special needs, LGBT, cohabitation, divorce, and alcohol and substance abuse. *If these situations do not apply, you can bypass this chapter.*

Special needs loved ones can be emotionally draining on a family. The specialized expertise required to manage their welfare varies by state. It is wise to include special needs professionals on your team if these circumstances apply to you.

Special circumstances require specialized thinking and planning ahead, especially when mentally, emotionally, physically, and chemically challenged people are involved. An advisor's role requires specific levels of knowledge and experience when dealing with these specific disabilities. The right advisor for your particular situation understands the laws and strategies required to navigate through a complicated and exhausting process. Special needs loved ones require qualified legal representation.

SPECIAL NEEDS FAMILIES

Families with special needs require sufficient income to care for family members with physical, mental, and emotional disabilities while simultaneously ensuring the welfare of all family members. A detailed budget should be prepared outlining the expenses of caring for the special needs person that considers the cost of inflation over their lifetime.

Expenses include medical care, special education support, physical, occupational or speech therapies; and adaptation of the home environment to their unique needs. Your goal is to assist loved ones with maintaining a high degree of independence and enjoying the life they deserve.

GOVERNMENT BENEFITS

A critical difference between traditional planning and special needs planning is access to government benefits. Government benefits for special needs people include access to residential and medical care facilities that may not be available through a private program, even if a client can afford to pay for them.

SPECIAL NEEDS TRUSTS (SNTS)

When you have unique or special needs to protect, trusts can play an important role.

A properly drafted Special Needs Trust can be created to provide for care and services not covered by government benefits. Generally, there are two types of SNT: First-Party Special Needs Trusts, and Third-Party Special Needs Trusts.

First-Party Trusts¶ hold assets belonging to the special needs person. Examples of these assets include personal injury awards, divorce settlements, life insurance proceeds, retirement plans and inheritances.

Third-Party Trusts** are trusts you create and fund with your own assets to helped a loved one with special needs. These can be current assets like investments or future assets like life insurance policies that will provide income after the caregivers are gone. These trusts may be funded with a variety of different assets, including life insurance.

A special needs attorney and an experienced insurance agent should be consulted to determine who the owner and beneficiary should be and if the use

¶. First-Party Trusts are governed by 42 U.S.C. Section 1396p(d)(3)(A).
**. Third-Party Trusts are governed by 42 U.S.C. Section 1396p(d)(3)(B).

of life insurance is appropriate for your specific circumstances.

IMPORTANCE OF TRUSTEES AND SUCCESSOR TRUSTEES

Trustees and successor trustees are people you entrust your children to after you are gone. They can include trusted family members, friends, corporate fiduciaries, an attorney, a CPA, a bank or a trust company. Consult your advisors about providing high quality care while preserving the ability to use government assistance programs when parents are no longer around. Trust planning is a complicated process that requires the assistance of subject matter experts. This type of planning will continue to evolve and change as laws change.

TITLING OF ASSETS CONSIDERATIONS

Titling of assets is a key component of asset protection planning. Depending upon your state, asset protection planning for dual spouse lawyers can be different than for individual lawyer asset protection planning. Titling is crucial because a creditor can only go after the assets of the specific person they have a judgment against.

Tenancy in the Entireties, which is a titling restricted inseparably to husband and wife. Each spouse owns these assets 100% and 100%.

Joint tenancy with the right of survivorship, is a titling that protects the surviving partner. Each owner owns their assets 50% and 50%. When one of the owners dies, the surviving owner gets the share of the partner who died.

Tenants in common are like a partnership in a particular asset. Each owner owns the assets 50% and 50%, and each owner can bequeath his or her share to anyone he or she wants to.

Special needs planning require an experienced lawyer and planner.

LESBIAN/GAY/BISEXUAL/TRANSGENDER (LGBT) PLANNING

The Supreme Court's June 26, 2015 ruling legalizing same-sex marriage in all 50 states has created a need for new planning. Due to the complexity of federal and state laws, special planning is required to protect the financial interests of LGBT parties. This area of the law requires specialized knowledge.

Estate Planning Considerations include Estate Administration, Estate Taxes, and Probate Issues.

Income tax considerations of assets upon death of each partner include unified tax credit and inheritance of Qualified Plans. Incapacitation would trigger the need for general power of attorney and healthcare power of attorney.

PLANNING CONSIDERATIONS
FOR LGBT COUPLES

As a married couple, you would benefit from both the unlimited marital deduction, which is restricted to legally married couples, and the portability of the first deceased spouse's unused estate tax exemption. For combined estates of over $10 million, if you purchase life insurance to pay estate taxes, you could benefit from purchasing a survivorship policy inside an Irrevocable Life Insurance Trust (ILIT) and be able to jointly fund the trust up to $28,000 per beneficiary per year through a gifting program, based on current tax law. This is a very complicated process. The exact amounts and guidelines are subject to IRS regulations. Seek subject matter experts regarding legal and tax advice prior to making any decisions.

SINGLE PARENT PLANNING

The single parent can be both the primary earner and caregiver for the children. These dual roles limit time available to address and protect financial interests, resulting in the need for additional planning and assistance to get the job done correctly. Potential issues include:

Family Dynamics: Are you single, married, divorced, or widowed?

Divorce Planning: Will you or your spouse be paying alimony?

Cash Flow Management: Who pays the bills now?

Estate Settlement Issues: If you passed away, who would administer your estate?

Birth of a Child: Who provides daily care for your child?

Child's Education: Who will pay for college and beyond?

Debt Management: Are you in debt and, if so, who is managing the repayment process?

Aging Parents: Will you be financially responsible for your parents' care some day?

Retirement: Are you able to save adequately for retirement?

Peace of mind: Is anything keeping you up at night?

COHABITATION

If a man and women want to live together without getting married, they should seek a qualified attorney and financial professional to map out their assets and plan distribution of those assets upon death of one of the partners. They should address their individual wills, trusts, healthcare directives, and powers of attorney with their attorney and professional team.

Additional issues to be considered include Social Security benefits, pension distributions, individual and joint credit obligations, beneficiary designations on life insurance policies, bank accounts and assets owned individually and jointly, inheritances related to children and grandchildren, or specific exclusion from inheritance.

If you intend to intentionally disinherit a family member, it is best to put a specific statement in your will or create a document that addresses your wishes. You cannot prevent litigation, but if it occurs, you will have created a document memorializing your intention.

DIVORCE PLANNING CONSIDERATIONS

With divorce statistics hovering at about 50%, "until death do us part" is no longer a reliable commitment for planning. Marriages exist with "my" children, "your" children, and "our" children. Planning can include prenuptial and post nuptials agreements.

A prenuptial agreement supersedes state marital law if prepared properly. Attorneys recommend that each party be represented by his or her own attorney, enter voluntarily into the agreement, prepare and complete the agreement well in advance of the wedding, and not include unreasonable, frivolous, or forbidding terms that would allow one party to negate the agreement after the fact.

Life insurance can protect alimony and child support payments and/or equalize distributions in the event of an untimely death. For estate planning purposes, special estate tax breaks exist only for married couples. If your personal estate is greater than the allotted amount for estate taxes, work with your advisors to minimize your heirs' taxable exposure.

If your income tax bracket drops substantially due to a divorce (because you are now filing separately), speak with your tax advisor about the pros and cons of converting any IRAs you have to a ROTH IRA.

PLANNING DOCUMENTS
FOR COLLEGE AGE CHILDREN

Once children reach the age of majority, as defined by each state, they are legal adults. At that point, a parent cannot make any financial or medical decisions for them. Parents can have their adult children establish a general power of attorney and a health care proxy. Have your child also sign a HIPAA release form allowing doctors to share medical information with designated people to ensure your children get proper and timely medical care should something happen to them.

ALCOHOL AND SUBSTANCE ABUSE

Addiction in the legal profession can be a serious issue. Legal professionals are subjected to life changing decisions, concerns about malpractice, long hours of work, debt due to student loans, and tremendous pressure from the decisions they are asked to make.

The impact of addiction on families can include loss of relationships, health, jobs, money, and possessions. Addicts can hurt or kill themselves and others. Addiction is a difficult problem that is rarely solved without expert intervention. Non-addicted family members are often locked unknowingly into roles and behavior patterns that reinforce the disease. An unbiased, impartial advisor should determine whether a case of addiction is an individual problem or a family problem before recommending treatment and appropriate support groups.

If you are in this situation, obtain the counsel of an attorney who specializes in this field of law.

If a spouse, child or loved one is going through substance abuse, consult your estate planning attorney to review your legal documents. Adjust these documents to address all the implications of having an addict as a trustee, successor trustee, or beneficiary of your estate. Additionally, if the people you have designated to raise your children become addicts or incapacitated, arrange for contingent or successor family members to raise them.

ASSISTED REPRODUCTIVE TECHNOLOGY (ART) PLANNING

While this topic may not apply to most people, ART is the next frontier of special needs planning. Technology creates issues and needs that never had to be addressed before. The ability to freeze eggs, sperm, and embryos has created numerous new legal implications for families and lawyers.

Consider this scenario: A husband and wife prepare reciprocal wills where a portion of their estate goes to their unborn child. The couple freezes and stores embryos and following the death of the husband, the wife remarries, then uses the frozen embryos and gives birth to a child after the first husband's death. Was the wife authorized by the husband to utilize this embryo after his death? Is this child now a beneficiary of the dead husband's estate? Is this child a beneficiary of any inheritances the dead husband would have received?

If you are in such a situation, speak with a trust and estate-planning attorney and also work with an attorney who specializes in ART planning.

THE HEALTH OF YOUR WEALTH SUMMARY
Promises Made; Promises Kept
It's All About Your Family

The capacity and skills required to serve a specialized market of legal families requires a deeper level of understanding career paths and the impact of future income stresses. Learning from your mistakes and others is a gift worth cherishing.

Wealth is what you accumulate,
not what you make or spend.

SECTION ONE: FOUNDATION OF WEALTH
Chapter 1: Your wealth team
1. How and whom you trust will be more important than the financial decisions you make.

2. No one player can win the game.

3. Balance your team with subject matter experts.

Chapter 2: Use trustworthy advisors

1. Advisors differ in experience, expertise, and agendas.

2. There are fiduciary, suitability, and transactional advisors.

3. Understand how your advisors work independently and as a team.

Chapter 3: Know what is getting in the way

1. Poor financial decisions can compound into a catastrophic event.

2. Second opinions are critical to catching poor financial decisions.

3. Learn from the mistakes of others.

Chapter 4: Cornerstones of planning

1. Risk management is critical.

2. You will be on and off track throughout your journey.

3. Every plan must lead to the achievement of your financial goals.

SECTION TWO: RISKS OF LIFE

Chapter 5: Risk Management

1. Understand the different types of risk.

2. Determine whether you can convert a serious risk into a manageable ongoing premium.

3. Ensure everything you cannot afford to lose, and partially or self insure everything else.

Chapter 6: Life Insurance

1. Own it or rent it.

2. Buy a death benefit and income loss protection, if you need it.

3. There are endless variations and designs of policies; choose wisely.

Chapter 7: DI Insurance

1. Definitions are critical to your coverage; choose wisely.

2. Riders should be evaluated and considered carefully.

3. Discounts can decrease your premiums considerably.

Chapter 8: LTC Insurance

1. Lock in your good health and pricing in your 50's and no later than early 60's.

2. Understand hybrid life/LTC products that are available.

3. Understand the impact of inflation on long term care planning.

SECTION THREE: LIFETIME PLANNING

Chapter 9: Lifetime Income Planning

1. Distribution planning is different than accumulation planning.

2. Put the appropriate retirement plans and investment allocation in place.

3. Make your goal to continuously deliver predictive and acceptable financial results.

Chapter 10: Special Situations

1. Special needs planning requires qualified, experienced professionals.

2. Trusts and titling are critical components of specialized planning.

3. Planning ahead is critical in preventing costly mistakes.

The most important question to ask every person who asks you to buy a service or a product:

How will this product integrate with all my other products, and help me achieve my strategic financial goals?

A trustworthy advisor should know the answer.

Learn about our workbook and workshops
available at
www.howardwolkowitz.com.

DEDICATION

To My Daddy, Morris Wolkowitz

My mother was agoraphobic; she never left the house. Our family rarely left the house, either. Our father was always there for us as both a mother and a father. He never complained. When he was not working, he enjoyed his three sons. His kids were his life and there was nobody he would rather be with.

At age 83, he started to become less sharp than we had known him to be. The crossword puzzle he did every day in the newspaper started to slide. Mail stacked up unopened. He would ask us the same question three times in five minutes. At first, my brothers and I would just say, "he's getting old." He was getting old, but he was also getting dementia.

As of this writing, he is 88. Even when a parent has a long-term care policy, a home health agency, and three loving sons, it is draining to watch that parent become a child because he can no longer take care of and protect himself.

Fortunately for our father, his unconditional commitment to his children inspired his children's unconditional commitment to him. I always called him "daddy," but never knew why until my daughter Cara said to me, "Daddy, anybody can be a dad, but not everybody can be a daddy."

I can say as a son, as a father, and as a grandfather, "Daddy, you took great care of us when we needed you. Now it's our turn to take great care of you when you need us."

Thank you, Daddy. Promises made; promises kept.

ABOUT THE AUTHOR

Howard Wolkowitz is an energetic visionary. He started his business career in banking in 1974. After 6 years, he decided that the best way to achieve financial security was to take control of his career and destiny by creating his own business. In 1992, Howard entered the financial services industry as a Financial Consultant.

In his 23 years as a Financial Consultant, Insurance Agent, and Financial Advisor, Howard noticed the mistakes people made as they navigated their financial lives. The mistakes centered around not having the knowledge to make wise decisions and/or not knowing whom to trust.

The foundation of financial wellbeing is that financial success is rarely achieved alone, but he noticed that few advisor professionals offer team-based, holistic guidance.

Howard decided to write a book showing professionals how to build teams around their financial needs. He created his own team of advisors with experience in wealth management, retirement, estate planning, income planning, insurance, annuities, employee benefits and special needs planning to meet the full spectrum of professionals' financial and insurance planning needs.

Howard Wolkowitz is a Registered Representative of MSI Financial Services, Inc., Member SIPC.

DISCLAIMER

This book was designed as a starting point for either hiring new advisors or working more effectively with your existing advisory team. This book is offered with the understanding and agreement that the author and publisher are not engaged in rendering legal, accounting, or other professional services through the book to the reader. The information is not written or intended, as tax or legal advice, and it may not be relied on for the purpose of avoiding any federal tax penalties. If legal or other expert assistance is required, the services of a competent professional should be sought. It is not the purpose of this book to present and cover the full body of knowledge of these many important topics. Every effort has been made to create an outline for discussion between you and your advisory team. You are accountable for your own due diligence. Use this book as a guide only; seek professional advice from experts.

Every effort has been made to make this book as complete and accurate as possible. However, there may be mistakes both typographical and in content regarding legal, tax, securities and financial matters. As this body of knowledge is vast and constantly changing, the content may only be current up to the time of printing.

The purpose of this book is to encourage the legal professional to seek his or her trustworthy advisors for advice and guidance. It also encourages trustworthy advisors to give to their clients and prospects, and to show their commitment and intention to operate at a higher level of service. The author and publisher of this book shall have neither liability nor responsibility to any person or entity with respect to any loss or damage caused, or alleged to have been caused, directly or indirectly, by the information contained in this program.

Read this book carefully and invest the time to adequately evaluate your own team of trustworthy advisors. You are solely responsible for creating your own team and making your own financial decisions.

The thoughts, views and opinions expressed herein are solely those of the author and do not reflect the views of his employer and his broker/dealer. This book is for informational purposes only and is not

ENDNOTES

1. (from p.68) The tax consequences are dependent on the policy not being a "modified endowment contract" (MEC) from being over funded. In general, policy owners may withdraw cash value equal to premiums paid without tax consequences although less favorable rules may apply in the earlier years of owning a policy. If the funding of the certificate exceeds certain limits, it will become a MEC and become subject to "earnings first" taxation on withdrawals and loans and an additional 10% penalty for withdrawals and loans taken before age 59½ will also generally apply. Your policy provider will notify you if a contribution would cause your policy to become a MEC. Withdrawals and loans reduce the death benefit and cash value, thereby diminishing the ability of the cash value to serve as a source of funding for cost of insurance charges, which may increase as you age. It is strongly suggested to seek professional guidance from your financial and tax advisor prior to taking any withdrawals or loans from a policy.

2. (from p.70) To purchase life insurance as an investment in addition to the death benefit, your ability to fund the policy above the cost of insurance needs to be carefully considered.

3. (from p.74) *Variable Universal Life Insurance is sold by prospectuses only. There will be a prospectus for the variable policy and individual prospectuses for the investment options available within the policy. The policy prospectus contains information about the product's features, risks, charges and expenses, and the investment objectives, risks and policies of the underlying investment options, as well as other information about the underlying investment option choices. Read the prospectuses and consider this information carefully before you invest or send money. Product availability and features may vary by state. All product guarantees are subject to the claims-paying ability of the issuing insurance company. Cash value allocated to the variable investment options is subject to market fluctuations so that, upon withdrawal or surrender, it may be worth more or less than the amount of premiums paid. There is no guarantee that any of the variable investment options will meet their stated goals or objectives.*

4. (from p.93) Cash value and death benefit will be reduced by the amount of any outstanding loan balance plus interest. Money borrowed does not participate in the investment performance of the policy. Unfavorable performance of a variable policy may necessitate the payment of additional premiums and without the payment of these additional premiums, the policy may lapse with significant tax consequences. Withdrawals may be subject to surrender charges and could have a permanent effect on the cash value and death benefit.

5. (from p.93) If the policy lapses due to a loan or withdrawal, it can reduce the cash value and the death benefit and maybe cause a taxable event.

6. (from p. 145) *Variable annuities are sold by prospectus only. Prospectuses for a variable annuity and for the investment options offered through the variable annuity are available from your financial representative. The contract prospectus will contain information about the contract's features, risks, charges and expenses. The investment objectives, risks and policies of the investment options, as well as other information about the investment options, are described in their respective prospectuses. Clients*

should read the prospectuses and consider this information carefully before investing.

There is no guarantee that any of the variable investment options in this product will meet their stated goals or objectives. The account value is subject to market fluctuations and investment risk so that, when withdrawn, it may be worth more or less than its original value, even when an optional protection benefit rider is elected. All contract and rider guarantees, including optional benefits and annuity payout rates, are subject to the claims-paying ability and financial strength of the issuing insurance company. Product availability and features may vary by state. Please refer to the contract prospectus for more complete details regarding the living and death benefits.

www.ingramcontent.com/pod-product-compliance
Lightning Source LLC
Chambersburg PA
CBHW031933190326
41519CB00007B/512